ALL SEVILLE

Photographs: Jorge Toledo, Alfonso Duran and Photographic Archives of FISA-Escudo de Oro.

Text, diagrams and reproduction conceived and carried
out in their entirety by the technical teams of
EDITORIAL FISA ESCUDO DE ORO, S.A.

⬦ ESCUDO DE ORO

S eville seduces for the artistic treasures it contains, which are not few, but mainly it attracts for its vital magic, something that you can only understand when you have lived in this city, even for only a few days, because it can be felt all around. In effect, the Sevillians have earned their fame of hedonists, gay and partying people, specially in events like the April Fair. They also have a deeply rooted worship for statues, that has its maximum expression during the Holy Week in Easter. But above all Seville is a cosmopolitan city, which enjoys the present and its traditions without forgetting the future, with the pleasure of doing it at their own pace without forgetting to fulfill the necessities and hurries of being a large city of southern Europe.

GEOGRAPHICAL INFORMATION AND HISTORICAL SUMMARY

The capital of Andalusia is situated by the banks of the Guadalquivir river, at the Southwest of the Iberian Peninsula, 10 meters above sea level. It has a mild climate –Mediterranean with oceanic influences–, and also with mild winters, pleasant temperatures in spring and autumn, and long hot summers. Presently it has 702,000 inhabitants, figure which converts it to the fourth most populated Spanish city, after Madrid, Barcelona and Valencia. The population of the province, with an extension of 14,001 km^2, is of 1,714,000 inhabitants.

Tradition attributes the foundation of Seville to Hercules, who after killing Gerion and stealing their oxen, marked with six stone pillars the place where Julius Caesar, in 45 BC, founded the Roman colony of *Iulia Romula Híspalis*.

GENERAL AERIAL VIEW. IN THE FIRST TERM, ESPAÑA SQUARE.

AERIAL VIEW OF THE CITY OF SEVILLE.

In honour to this legend those six pillars were identified centuries later with six Roman columns which remained of a temple raised during the 2nd century in the Street of the Marmoles: two of the columns were moved to the Alameda de Hercules Avenue when opened in 1574, and finished off with statues of Hercules and Julius Caesar, other three columns still remain in the mentioned street and it seems that the sixth column broke down and was lost. Within a more scientifical basis we know

that in this area flourished the fabulous kingdom of Tartessus, from which we possess the so called Treasure of the Carambolo, found at the outskirts of the city in 1958 and which is exposed at the Archaeological Museum. Phoenicians and Greeks opened up trade links with the Tartessians, and it was their descendants who, towards the 8th century BC, established a settlement by the banks of the Gualdalquivir called Ispal which can be considered the origin of Seville.

In the 3rd century BC the Carthaginians occupied the area, but the rivalry of these with the Romans during the second Punic War forced the Legions of Scipio the African to disembark in Spain, achieving to defeat at Ilipa, near Ispal, in 206 B.C, the Carthaginian general Asdrubal. The winner Scipio then founded the city of Italica, 10 km from Ispal, for the retirement of his troops. Both settlements, the now called Hispalis and Italica, experimented periods of great splendour, specially since when in 45 BC Julius Caesar gave Hispalis the category of Roman colony, turning to be one of the most important cities, not only of Andalusia, but of whole Hispania. Even so, nowadays in Seville there are very few remains left of the Roman period. On the other hand in Italica visitors can find excellent vestiges, such as a theatre, an amphitheatre and rests of mosaics.

During the expansion of Christianity in the Peninsula, we have to mention the holy Sevillians Justa and Rufina, patron Saints of the city and of the potters and ironmongers. These Saints were sisters and they earned their living selling clay pots in the street. One day, towards 287, in a pagan procession, they denied a requested donation confessing their Christian faith, therefore their pottery was destroyed but the two sisters broke the pagan image, for what they had to suffer martyrdom.

The Roman period was followed by the invasions of Vandals, Swabians and Visigoths. With these last ones, during the 6th and 7th centuries, Seville became again one of the main cultural focuses of the western world. Saint Isidore (560-635), archbishop of Seville and author of "Etymologies", encyclopedia which collects all the knowledge of the period, and his brother Leander were the most known personalities of the time.

The Arab domination, which supposed a new period of splendour, began in 712. The city changed its name to Isbiliah and the river Betis was called Guad el Kevir ("the big river"), words which give origin to their present names. Although at the beginning the center of power was established in Cordoba, Seville standed out for its own reasons, achieving special relevance with the arrival in 1147 of the Almohades, who

ROMAN COLUMNS IN THE MÁRMOLES STREET.

SANTIPONCE: RUINS OF THE AMPHITHEATER OF ITÁLICA.

"Saints Justa and Rufina", work of Goya of 1817 (Cathedral of Seville).

Portrait of Ferdinand III the Saint, of Murillo (Cathedral of Seville).

established their capital in this city. To this last period of Arabic-Andalusian dominion correspond buildings like the Giralda (which was the minaret of the great mosque), the Torre del Oro (Tower of the Gold), the fortress (later rebuilt by the Christian Monarchs) or the walls of the Macarena.

In 1248, after two years of siege, Ferdinand III the Saint conquered Seville to Christendom. The Muslims were obliged to leave, staying only the Hebrews and the Mudejars, resettling the city at the same time with about 24,000 Castillians: the first ones were installed in the present quarters of Santa Cruz and San Bartolome, and the Castillians in congregations or parishes depending to which guild they belonged to the rest of the city. This event

gave origin to the fact that each guild had their own devoted Saint, and so generating the phenomenon of the brotherhood associations. The mosques were converted into churches and other new ones were founded and also many convents. Another action of the monarch was to establish the court of the Kingdom of Castile in the fortress, which will become the first Spanish Royal House. Ferdinand III stayed in Seville until his death in 1252 and since then he is considered the patron Saint of the city. His remains rest in a silver urn in the Royal Chapel of the Cathedral. This king is also the main character in the city's shield, in which he is flanked by the Sevillian bishops Isidore and Leander.

The work commenced by Ferdinand III

was continued by his son Alfonso X the Wise, whose tolerant kingdom allowed the flowering of the Jewish, Arab and Christian knowledge. We also owe Alfonso X the peculiar emblem that can be read in many places of the city and in various versions of the shield of Seville. It is the cryptogram NO8DO, composed of two syllables divided by a kind of a interweaved hank and which corresponds to the phonetical expression in Spanish of the phrase "the city has not left me" (in Spanish "no me ha dejado"). This phrase refers to the loyalty the city showed the king during a clash between him and his son Don Sancho. During the kingdom of Peter I of Castile (1350-69), known with the nickname of *The Cruel*, but known in Seville as *The Avenger*, the city grew extraordinarily. Among the buildings, he rebuilt the Arab fortress, which was converted in an exquisite Mudejar palace. Still today many streets of the old quarter recall with their names love stories and crimes in which this monarch was involved and whose kingdom was marked by the conflict that faced him with his stepbrother Henry of Trastamara, who killed him and with whom began a new dynasty.

In 1401, in the place where the major mosque stood, of which is conserved the minaret (the Giralda) and the ablutions patio (nowadays called Patio of the Orange trees), began the construction of the cathedral, essentially gothic, which will become the biggest in dimensions in Spain. Nevertheless, until the so called period of the discoveries the architectural style that defines the city is the Mudejar one, which has in the mentioned Royal Fortress and in the House of Pilate (from the beginning of the 16th century) its best exponents. During the 15th century it reached its culmination in 1492, when Granada was taken, and with which the process of the Reconquest finished (that same year the Catholic Monarchs also ordered the expulsion of the Jews from their Kingdom and established in Seville the see of the Holy Inquisition) and also the year of the discovery of America. This last happening meant to Seville a period of apogee, as here was established the House of Contracts, the commercial organisation which monopolized the commercial relationships with the

FACADE OF THE PALACE OF THE KING DON PEDRO (ROYAL FORTRESS' OF SEVILLE). LITHOGRAPH ACCORDING TO A DRAWING OF GIRAULT DE PRANGEY (1837).

THE UNIVERSITY, OLD TOBACCO FACTORY.

possessions of overseas. The economical wealth created by the new American market turned Seville in to the wealthiest, most prosperous and cosmopolitan city of Spain, at the same time as the country, as a result of the coronation in 1519 of Charles V as emperor of the Holy Roman Germanic Empire, raised to be the most powerful nation of Europe, although on the other hand, the continuous wars of the Empire consumed large part of the wealth that arrived to the harbour of Seville. The urban development of the city went through a thorough transformation, passing the limits of the walls and baroque forming in its most representative architectural style. The population also grew at an unstoppable pace, reaching 150,000 inhabitants at the end of the 16th century. The city received the most distinguished artists of the moment and saw the birth of painters like Velázquez (1599), Murillo (1617) and Valdés Leal (1622).

The terrible plague which the city suffered in 1649, managed to reduce the population in half, and the covering in mud of the river Guadalquivir in 1680, as a result of which the fleet of the In-

SANTA JUSTA TRAIN STATION.

dies was moved to the harbour of Cádiz (the definitive move of the House of Contracts to Cádiz was done in 1717) meant the beginning of a decline for Seville which tried to resist to loose the prominence of its glorious past. The city did maintain some commercial monopoly, like the one of tobacco, for which an immense factory was built, nowadays as building of the University, and immortalized by Prosper Merimée in his famous novel *Carmen*. At the beginning of the 19th century Seville still should suffer another plague and see how, as a result of the French occupation during the Independence War, the troops of marshal Soult took great part of the rich artistic patrimony that existed in churches and convents.

During the Isabella period Seville knew a certain prosperity. As for urban reforms we have to mention the construction of the bridge of Isabella II in 1845 and the opening of new squares and streets after demolishing the walls in 1869. It was also in this period when the famous April Fair was born (1848). The more recent history of the city is determined for the celebration of two exhibitions. With the first one, the Latin American Exhibition of 1929, created to promote the Andalusian economy, Seville saw part of its appearance transformed with various buildings of the so called regionalistic architecture, specially concentrated in the Park of María Luisa, which was the premises of the exhibition. With the second one, the Universal Exhibition of 1992, Seville opened to the future and obtained a new urban profile of modernist style, visible essentially at the other side of the Guadalquivir, in the called Isle of La Cartuja.

THE GIRALDA AND THE FRONT OF THE CATHEDRAL.

TWO IMAGES OF THE PROCESSION OF THE SAN BENITO FRATERNITY.

PENITENTS.

FESTIVITIES
The Holy Week

The Sevillian Holy Week enjoys of a gained universal renown. The fact that it coincides with the splendour of spring gives to these original and intense religious festivities a pleasant natural frame and of incomparable beauty. It is, with no doubt, an unforgettable spectacle, in which art and fervour are closely associated. Apart from being a religious event of great significance, the Holy Week acquires in Seville a social significance, since quarters and trades are integrated in the brotherhoods, from the most humble to the highest Sevillian social strata.

The first itinerary of the Sevillian brotherhoods began in 1520, from the Chapel of the House of Pilate to the Mudejar temple of Cruz del Campo. At this point ended a station of one kilometer, in other words, the same distance that Jesus walked from the Pretory of Pilate to the Calvary, in the Holy Land.

Presently there are in Seville about

fifty brotherhoods, which walk a total of a hundred steps. The processions take place every day during the Holy Week –each day pass along seven or eight brotherhoods– in the afternoon and night, while the route lasts about twelve hours. The processions start in the churches where the brotherhoods have their headquarters to arrive up to the Cathedral and going back by a different route. Each brotherhood, which dresses up with a distinctive costume, usually march in two floats, sculptural groups that represent in the first one an image of the Passion and in the second one an image of Our Lady of Sorrows. The floats are carried on their shoulders by the 'costaleros' to the rythm that marks the voice of a foreman. The 'nazarenos' or penitents which accompany them have their heads covered by a kind of pointed hood and a big candle in their hands.

The brotherhoods carry out in procession very old images and of great artistical value, among them the Christ Burgos –an image sculpt in the 16th century by Juan Bautista Vázquez–, the Christ of the Students –by Juan de Mesa–, Jesus of the Passion –with his layette of 200 kilograms of filigree silver, by Martínez Montañés–, and the

PROCESSION OF THE STUDENTS FRATERNITY..

PROCESSION OF THE SAN GONZALO FRATERNITY.

Virgin of Macarena –attributed to Luisa Roldán–, whose extraordinary beauty dazzles the Sevillians and has converted her in a deeply popular image.

The oldest brotherhood is the one called the Brotherhood of the Silence (Cofradía del Silencio), which is dated from 1356. It is called so because its rules don't allow the penitents to talk. The most popular brotherhood in, with no doubt, the one of the Macarena, whose lovely image arouses in people such a passionate feeling, that sometimes it almost seems as profane as religious. From two o'clock in the afternoon of Palm Sunday until the night of Easter Sunday, the streets of Seville, that smell intensely to wax, incense and orange blossoms, are transcended of religiousness to the passing by of the images, and the people mill around and get excited as the sacred procession develops. Finally, a jubilant tolling of bells extends through the air as culmination of the Holy Week, announcing Easter.

PROCESSION OF THE SANTA GENOVEVA FRATERNITY.

THE VIRGIN OF GRACIA AND AMPARO IN PROCESSION.

DIFFERENT ASPECTS OF THE APRIL FAIR.

The April Fair

It is considered the Andalusian fair par excellence and it has universal fame. Its origin is dated in 1292, when Alfonso X the Wise bestowed the city with the historical Concession Letter which authorized the celebration of two fairs, the "Cincuesma" and the "Saint Michael" one. Nevertheless, the April Fair does not achieve real naturalization papers, specially in the stockbreeding and agricultural aspects, until Elizabeth II, in 1847, renewed and approved with her signature the medieval document. The fair is celebrated during the second half of April and it last one week. A great entrance arch illuminated with many lights give way to a sort of improvised city with hundreds of canvas stands with colourful stripes, that aline in artificial streets decorated with colourful Chinese lanterns. The fiesta normally starts on a Monday at mid night with the lighting of the great entrance arch and ends on Sunday with fireworks.

To the April Fair come people from all around Andalusia, from Spain –we could say that from all around the world-, to take part of the joy, friendliness, gracefulness and good humour the Sevillians radiate continuously at all times. It is very characteristic of this fiesta that women dress up with the typical 'faralaes' costume and men with a short typical suit, for horseriding. The gay Sevillian dynamism is present everywhere, in the Jerez wine that is filled with by the typical "catavinos", in the playing of the guitar, in the hand clapping and heel clicking of the "bailaores" and "bailaoras" dancers, in the Sevillian dances that can go out until dawn, in the rides of the horsemen and in the harnessed horses.

DIFFERENT ASPECTS OF THE PROCESSION OF EL ROCÍO.

The Procession of El Rocío

After the April Fair, the most popular and important of the Sevillian fiestas, is the Procession of El Rocío. A peregrination of pilgrims of all social classes that goes to the chapel that is raised in the marshes of the river Guadalquivir, not far from Almonte, in the province of Huelva. This fiesta is celebrated at the end of May or beginnings of June and the participants arrive mainly from the provinces of Seville, Huelva and Cádiz, being the number of persons from Seville the largest. The route from Seville has 95 km and it is done by carriages pulled by oxen, riding a horse or walking. In the carriages, decorated with garlands, cluster together the young ladies with their typical costumes, while men –with a loose lightweight shirt, long johns, leather chaps and a wide brimmed hat– ride horses of all kinds, carrying in the rump ladies with the typical dress with the shawl tied up in their waist. On Pentecost Saturday they arrive to the chapel and the presentation is done to the Virgin of Rocío, the "White Dove" ("Blanca Paloma"), faithfully guarded by the Brotherhood of Matriz de Almonte. On Sunday a High Mass is held and at night the public Rosary. At early hours of Monday the people from the village of Almonte, the only ones that have this privilege, jump over the railings to take the Virgin out in procession. The crowd bursts to claim the Virgin and rush towards her to try to touch the silver rods.

BULL TAIL, "GAZPACHO" AND PASTRY CRAFTS.

GASTRONOMY AND CRAFTWORKS

The Sevillian people, without being greedy, is very fond of fine and select cuisine. Also in their typical way of eating the innate gracefulness of the Sevillian people is reflected, so keen to the "tapas" and going out for a few glasses of wine. It is not difficult for them, in more than one occasion, to substitute conventional lunch or dinner for a few "chatos" (glasses of wine) with their corresponding "tapas", that go from the delicious Sevillian olives to fried fish, including in between small filet of meat, the soldiers of Pavía (slices of fried codfish battered with flour), the croquettes or ox tail.

Two very popular dishes of the Sevillian cuisine are the "gazpacho" and the Andalusian stew. The first one is light and refreshing and the second one, thick and overelaborated. Also dishes of exquisite palate are the "menudo" (tripes), seafood dishes and wild asparagus Andalusian style.

In the varied and suggestive chapter of the Sevillian confectionery we have to mention the "yemas de San Leandro" (sweets made with egg yolk and sugar), the "Santa Inés buns", the "polvorones" (floury sweet made with almonds), the oil cakes, the "mostachones", and the "cortadillos" stuffed with citron. It would be a never ending story to name them all, while Seville offers temptations for all tastes.

As to the craftworks, nowadays there still are many workshops whose work methods have maintained almost the same as in days gone by, thanks mainly to the demand of the various brotherhoods. In the embroidery technique, done with silk, gold, silver and copper threads, the tradition goes back to the 15th century, time from which there is proof of a guild dedicated to this art. The Sevillian goldsmith art has given brilliant samples: the Custody of Arfe is the master work, but the city itself, with its artistical grilles, is a good indicator of it. Ceramics have great importance since antiquity. In this sense, is very characteristic the retable of tiles in the external wall of the church, representing the image that is kept inside. On the other hand, we must not forget the woodcarvers and gilders, with great masters throughout history.

The most typical shopping one can do in Seville are the fans (made of wood and handpainted), the lace mantillas embroided by hand, typical dress of "faralaes", guitars, conventual products such as the "yemas de San Leandro", Santa Inés buns and the marmalades of the convent of Santa Paula, and, of course, ceramics from Triana.

CRAFTSMEN WORKSHOPS OF EMBROIDERY AND ENGRAVING.

VIRGEN DE LOS REYES SQUARE AND THE ENCARNACIÓN CONVENT.

Both squares, adjoining, represent the heart of the monumental Seville, since there we can find its three main historical buildings, declared Heritage of the Humanity by the UNESCO in 1987: the Cathedral with its unmistakable tower of the Giralda, the Royal Fortresses and the Archive of the Indies. We neither miss in both squares the classical horse carriages and other cliché aspects such as gypsies selling flowers or telling your fortune. In the first square, besides of the Giralda and the backside facade of the Cathedral, other two buildings stand out, the Archbishop's Palace and the Convent of the Encarnación, and in its centre there stands a spectacular **streetlight** from the beginnings of

the 20th century, done by José Lafita, with a fountain in its base.

The **Archbishop's Palace**, built between the 16th and 17th centuries, has a facade that is, for the graceful rhythm of its elements and for its intense colours (purple and ocher-yellow), one of the best examples of the Sevillian baroque. The inside keeps various interesting elements, like a staircase of jasper and paintings of Zurbarán, Murillo, Herrera the Old and Valdés Leal. The artistic richness of the palace was much bigger in days gone by, but it was very damaged when converted in headquarters of the Napoleonic troops during the Independence War, as well as many of its pictures were taken away by marshal

Soult at the end of the conflict and today they form part of French and English museums.

The **Convent of the Encarnación**, of white walls and of much more simple making, was built at the end of the 14th century in the site of an ancient mosque. The church has a neoclassical retable and paintings and sculptures of the 17th and 18th centuries. In the outside, a plaque reminds that in this place existed the Corral de los Olmos, a dating place of the rogues recalled by Miguel de Cervantes in many of his books. Following the walls of the church, to the left, an alley brings you to the peaceful **Santa Marta Square**, one of the most enchanting places of Seville.

ARCHBISHOP'S
PALACE.

SANTA MARTA SQUARE.

A **monument to Santa Inmaculada** stands out at the **Triunfo Square**, by Collaut Valera, which was raised to mark the proclamation of the dogma of Santa Inmaculada Concepción. The square, however, owes its name to the **monument of the Triunfo**, next to the Archive of the Indies, built in thanksgiving for having overcome without suffering the city from major damages of the earthquake in Lisbon in 1755. The monument is raised exactly where a mass celebrated in honour of All Saints was concluded after being interrupted by the seismic movements.

TRIUNFO SQUARE.

MONUMENT
OF THE
TRIUMPH.

The most emblematic monument of Seville, and one of the most admired towers of the world, is the old minaret of the great mosque in which place was raised the Cathedral in the 15th century. Its construction was ordered in 1171 by the Almohade sultan Abu Yacub Yusuf and finished by his son in 1198, the emir Abu Yusuf Yacub al-Mansur. The architect who designed the tower was Aben Baso, although the inspection of the works was in charge of a poet, Abubequer Benzoar, which would explain, into a certain point, the existence of that halo of delicate fantasy that emanates from the original and slender architecture of the Giralda. The tower, which had 82 meter of height, was finished with four big overplaced golden copper globes that with the sun must have shown very far. From there the muezzin called the faithful to prayer, but probably it was also used as an astrological observatory. To climb to the top, instead of stairs 35 ramps of gentle ascent were done. It seems this was done to provide access to the horse of the first muezzin of the minaret, who was a very old man.

The legends says that when the Muslim chiefs negotiated the surrender of Seville in 1248, these asked to destroy the great mosque and its minaret to avoid them to get in hands of the Christians. But when such demand got to the attention of the then prince Don Alfonso, he threatened to kill anybody who would dare to remove one of its bricks and destroy such a beautiful building. In 1355, because of an earthquake, three of the four golden globes collapsed. They were replaced with simple Christian symbols until 1558 when

NOCTURNAL VIEW FROM THE GIRALDA FROM THE TRIUNFO SQUARE.

Hernán Ruiz received the order of a new finish. The architect finished the tower, the one we can contemplate today, in 1568, gaining in height up to 103 meters. It consists of four Renaissance bodies which where provided with bells and the colossal crowning of the Triumph of the Faith in Christ (Triunfo de la Fe en Cristo). The fact that this crowning turns around moved by the wind became the origin of the popular name of the monument, since the Sevillians started to call it 'giralda' (word in Span-

ish for a weather vane finished by a human or an animal figure).

The best perspective of the Giralda is obtained from the Mateos Gago Street, although its presence in the city is constant, almost ubiquitous. The tower appears, totally or partially, from the most unexpected urban angles. From its high viewpoint, you can see a broad landscape of the city, of the Andalusian countryside, with its white farmhouses and its green gardens and the calm flow of the Gualdalquivir.

PERSPECTIVE OF THE GIRALDA FROM THE VIRGEN DE LOS REYES SQUARE.

The Cathedral of Seville is the biggest temple of Spain and third of the Christian world, only exceeded in extension by the Basilica of Saint Peter in Rome and the Saint Paul's Cathedral in London. In this sense, it reflects perfectly the ambitious enthusiasm of who designed and decided the construction of this building, somewhere at the end of the 14th century, this phrase appears in some chapters: "Let us make such and so big temple, that those who will see it finished will consider us insane". The interior floor of the temple occupies a rectangle of 116 meters of length times 76 meters of width, and the highest point of the crossing reaches the height of 56 meters. Although the fundamental work of the building was done between 1401 and 1506, four centuries were necessary to achieve the profile it has currently. It consists of five naves, being the one in the middle the highest and widest, and it does not have a nave that goes around the apse, in its place there is a passage which serves of division between the Main Chapel and the Royal Chapel. As a whole it impresses not only for its dimensions, but also for the solidity and excellence of the building, and also for the inestimable value of the artistic heritage it keeps inside.

Of the great mosque on top of which the cathedral was built were conserved the minaret (la Giralda) and the Patio of the Orange Trees, which corresponds to the old ablutions patio. Encircles the cathedral's premises the popular **"gradas"**, steps protected by a row of columns connected by chains. Their origin goes back to 1392, when they were built to serve as a contracting point of labourers due to a very precarious year for the agriculture. Soon

AERIAL VIEW OF THE CATHEDRAL.

DOOR OF THE PRINCE OR OF SAN CRISTÓBAL.

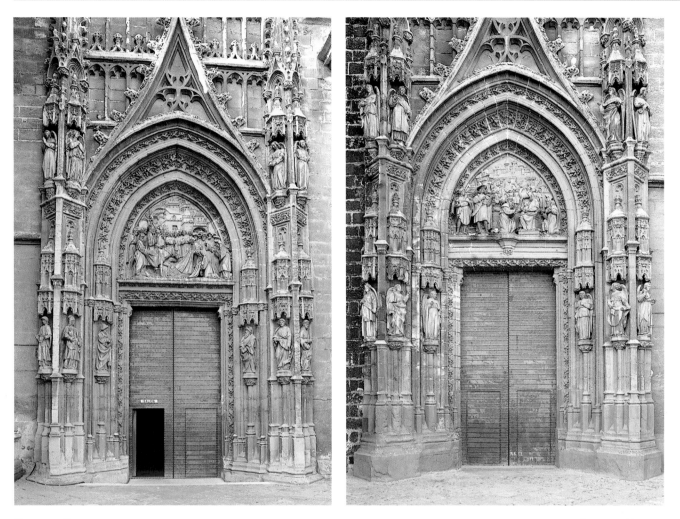

DOOR OF CAMPANILLAS.

DOOR OF PALOS.

they became a regular place for commercial exchanges, developing a feverish activity specially after the discovery of America. People of all kind and of all places came to this spot in search of a job or to carry out their commercial deals, which afterwards were formalized in the House of Contracts, located very near of the fortress; in case of rain or of excessive heat many used to continue their negotiations inside the Cathedral, for what reason the ecclesiastical Council stipulated to surround the temple with chains. The solution, however, came with the con-

struction in 1572 of the Guildhall House of the Merchants (today Archive of the Indies). The chains also limited the right of asylum of the church in front of the justice, the same way as if someone remained inside the temple, and so it was until very recent dates.

The cathedral's premises has nine doors, of different periods and artistic making. The **main facade**, in the Constitution Avenue, presents three doors: the main door, also called of the Asunción, from the 19th century, and the Baptistery and Birth doors,

both from the 15th century and profusely decorated with fired clay figures. In the South wall is located the **Door of San Cristóbal**, finished in the 19th century. In the back facade, both sides of the gothic apse, we find the **Door of Campanillas** and the **Door of Palos**, this last one next to the Giralda. Both were decorated in the 16th century by Miguel Florentín. In the North wall we find one of the most interesting doors, the **Door of Forgiveness**, which communicates with the Patio of the Orange Trees. The leaves of the door, made of larch and covered with copper, pres-

ent a bow decoration and Arabic Kufa inscriptions and they conserve the two doorknockers of the Almohade period. The sculptures of Saint Peter and Saint Paul and of the group of the Annunciation are owed to Miguel Florentín, and the decoration of the plateresque plasterwork, also from the 16th century, to Bartolomé López. The two last doors are located inside of the premises and they communicate the Patio of the Orange Trees with the interior of the temple. One is the **East Door**, also called of Concepción and of the Orange Trees, done in the 20th century by Casanova in Gothic style, and the other one is the **Door of the Lizard**, name which refers to a crocodile of natural size that hangs from the arch, replica in wood of one dissected, apparently a gift of the sultan of Egypt to Alfonso X.

The sensation one has when entering the Cathedral of Seville is incredible, as the grandeur of the building moves. In the central nave, behind the retro-choir and the **choir**, this one with a splendid Gothic chair work and organs from the 17th century, stands out the **Main Chapel**, closed by a magnificent plateresque grille of golden iron. The immense retable which is its prevalent figure is a master piece of the florid Gothic and maximum treasure of the temple. In this huge retable (of 20 meters of height times 13 meters of width, the biggest one of Christendom) participated practically all the artists of the city. The original design

CHOIR OF THE CATHEDRAL.

PLATERESQUE ▶ GRILLE OF THE MAIN CHAPEL.

RETABLE OF
THE MAIN
CHAPEL.

corresponds to Pierre Dancart and it was done between 1482 and 1533. It adds up a total of 45 panels with more than a thousand figures, dealing with scenes of the Old and New Testament. The Virgin of the Sede, Gothic sculpture of the 14th century, occupies a place of honour.

The **Royal Chapel** is of Renaissance-Plateresque trace and the coffered ceiling of the beautiful dome was designed by Hernán Ruiz. In the Royal Chapel we find the royal tombs of Alfonso X the Wise and his mother, Beatrice of Suabia, and, in a rich silver urn, the mortal rests of the king Ferdinand. In the crypt that is behind we find the coffins of Peter I the Cruel and his wife, María de Padilla. In the altar stands out the image of the Virgin of the Kings (Virgen de los Reyes), patron saint of the city, sculpture of the 13th century. Every 15 of August this image, for who the Sevillians feel great devotion, is carried in procession in the very early hours of the morning around the Cathedral in front a silent crowd that is concentrated to contemplate her while she passes by. According to the tradition, while she comes out, the Virgin concedes the three desires that she has been demanded.

In the **Main Sacristy** is shown the **treasure** of the cathedral. Remarks a huge triangular candelabra, worked by Morel and Hernán Ruiz, and the big monstrance of Arfe, a unique piece of the Renaissance goldsmithing. This exquisite piece comes out in procession the day of Corpus Christi, day on which also takes place the dance of the popular *Seises* in front of the main altar. The dance looks very similar to a slow *minuet*, and the peculiarity is that it is interpreted by children dressed up in old fashioned style.

The **Sacristy of the Chalices** shows painting of Goya (*Saints Justa and*

ROYAL CHAPEL: URN OF SAN FERNANDO AND IMAGE OF THE VIRGEN DE LOS REYES.

MAIN SACRISTY.

Rufina), Zurbarán (*Virgin with Child and Crucified*) and Valdés Leal (*Liberation of Saint Peter*), and in the altar stands out one of the main work of art of the Sevillian baroque making of religious figures, the *Christ of the Mercy*, done by Martínez Montañés in 1603.

In the **Chapterhouse**, with an elliptical floor, designed by Hernán Ruiz, attracts attention the marbles sculpt by Marcos Cabrera and the pictorial group of the vault, painted in 1668 by Murillo, presided by an image of Santa Inmaculada Concepción.

THE SEISES DANCE.

CHAPTERHOUSE AND MAUSOLEUM OF CHRISTOPHER COLUMBUS.

In front of the door of San Cristobal is the **mausoleum of Cristopher Colombus**, composition of Arturo Melida from 1900 in which four pages with the shields of Castile, Navarra, León and Aragón hold up the coffin.

Near the Door of Baptism we can admire the genuine **Giraldillo** or the statue of the Faith of Giralda, installed here due to the latest restoration works of the tower, being a copy of the original the one that crowns it.

We have to mention also the **stained glass windows** and, definitely, a great many wonderful works of art that the cathedral of Seville stores in its several **chapels**. We have to mention the retable of the Virgin de la Antigua, with an image of her from the 14th century; the tomb of cardinal Cervantes, done in alabaster by Lorenzo Mercadante in 1458, in the chapel of San Hermenegildo; the paintings of Murillo *The Vision of San Antonio of Padua* and *The guardian angel*, the first one in the chapel of San Antonio and the second one near the main door, the delicate image of the Virgin of Bethlehem in the chapel of the same name, done by Alonso Cano in 1635; and

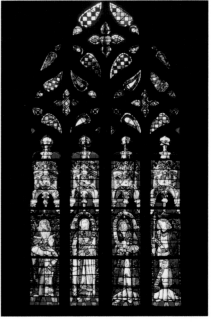

STAINED GLASS WINDOWS OF THE CENTRAL NAVE.

TOMB OF CARDINAL CERVANTES.

the retable painted by Zurbarán in the chapel of San Pedro.

The **Patio of the Orange Trees (Patio de los Naranjos)** is today a peaceful garden which amazes for its simple beauty. It has a central fountain, whose basin is originally from a Visigothic cathedral, and a stone pulpit from where preached, among others, Juan de Avila, Francisco de Borja and Vicente Ferrer. Above the nave called nave of the Lizard is situated the **Colombina Library**, founded in 1551, with a valuable and extensive collection of manuscripts donated by the son of Christopher Columbus, Domenico Columbus. In the West side of the patio is the **Sagrario church**, built in the 17th century as a cathedral chapel and converted later into a parish. Of interest we can find there a retable with sculptures of Pedro Roldán dealing with the Descent from the Cross, moving for its great realism, and huge statues of the Evangelists and Fathers of the Church by Juan de Arce.

"THE GUARDIAN ANGEL", PAINTING OF MURILLO.
DOOR OF FORGIVENESS FROM THE PATIO OF THE ORANGE TREES.

GENERAL ARCHIVE OF THE INDIES.

The building of the General Archive of the Indies, of sober Renaissance style, has a square floor, two stores and a central patio with an arcade. It was raised between 1584 and 1598, according to the drawings of Juan de Herrera, to accommodate the Guildhall of the Merchants and so being able to clear the intensive commercial activity that was carried out in the neighbourhood's House of Contracts and in the steps of the Cathedral caused by the discovery of America. As headquarters of the Archive of the Indies it was founded in 1785 by Charles III to centralize the extensive and valuable documentation in relationship with the Spanish possessions overseas, until then spread in various buildings. Today it is one of the world's most important archives. It is calculated that it contains about 86 million manuscript pages and more than 8.000 plans and drawings dated between the 15th and 19th centuries. Among the most important appear the World Map of Juan de la Cosa and the Diary of Christopher Columbus. There also are kept letters of Hernán Cortés, Cervantes, and even of George Washington, first president of the United States. In the exhibition halls and in the library are exposed drawings and maps of different periods, some of them very curious.

DOOR OF THE LION.

The Royal Fortresses (Reales Alcázares) are called so, in plural, because it includes a group of buildings, from the primitive Arab fortress to the following extensions of patios and palaces that were built by successive monarchs. From the fortress raised by the Almohades in the 12th century only a part of the walls remain, Patio del Yeso and the Patio de la Montería. Its present structure responds in great measure to the reform done by Peter I the Cruel, who, nevertheless, used many of the elements of the original constructions.

You can reach the grounds through the **Door of the Lion (Puerta del León)**, opened in the Almohade walls. To the left is the **Justice Room**, remain of the old fortress created by Alfonso XI beside the beautiful **Patio del Yeso**. Then you can reach **Patio de la Montería**, which was the old *mexuar*, a space used as anteroom that separated the city from the palace. The distribution of the primitive fortress followed the classical scheme of the Arab palaces, with a space dedicated to the public life, around the Patio de las Doncellas, and a second space reserved to the private life, around the Patio de las Muñecas; a big fortified garden completed the whole.

COFFERED CHAMFER OF THE JUSTICE ROOM.

In the Patio de la Montería impresses the magnificent facade of **the Palace of King Don Pedro**, main work of the Mudejar art. It was built in the 14th century and it was done with the participation of local artists and of nazaries artists that came from Granada apart from carpenters from Toledo. It presents an exquisite decoration, with Gothic and Arab inscriptions of Kufa, a reflection of the crossing of the cultures of the period. Of the different rooms of the top floor stands out the called **oratory of the Catholic Mon-** **archs**, a small chapel whose altar made of glazed tiles, done by Niculoso Pisano in 1503, is a main piece of the ceramics of Seville, cause it represented an innovation in the art of tile glazing. From the Patio de la Montería, a hall gives way to the **Patio of the Maidens (Patio de las Doncellas)**, of grand spaciousness and luminosity. Its walls are covered with glazed tiles, with no doubt being one of the most beautiful of the palace. The top floor was added in the 16th century. The fine columns present extravagant stucco orna-

PATIO DE LA MONTERÍA: FACADE OF KING DON PEDRO'S PALACE.

ARCHES OF
THE PATIO
OF THE
MAIDENS.

HALL OF AMBASSADORS.

mentation and we have to outstand also the wooden artscraft. Recent excavations have revealed, under its floor, a patio with a central water deposit, longitudinal with two gardens and with ornamental details of notable making, a very interesting design since there does not exist any another similar one of this period in the city nor in the rest of the world.

The Patio de las Doncellas connects with the **Charles V Hall**, in where stands out a Renaissance coffering. Adjoined

DOME OF THE HALL OF AMBASSADORS.

PATIO OF
THE DOLLS.

TAPESTRIES HALL.

are the rooms of María de Padilla, wife of king Peter I. From here we have access to a dining room of the period of Ferdinand II and to the splendid **Hall of Ambassadors (Salón de Embajadores)**. Its construction was ordered by Peter I the Cruel and virtually so it has stayed until nowadays; only the balconies were added in the 16th century. The walls, the arches and the door frames are covered by a brilliant Mudejar decoration. The hall is crowned by a great Mozarabic dome of the 15th century, although restored

in later occasions. In the Gallery of the Kings of Spain are represented from Recadero to Philip II, monarch who established the capital of the kingdom in Madrid.

Through the Bedroom of Philip II we reach the **Patio of the Dolls (Patio de las Muñecas)**, a private patio full of singular grace around which the private life of the palace was carried out. The plinth, the columns and the capitals are of their original period, while the upper part is from the 19th century. The patio connects with the

Bedroom of Isabella I of Castile, the Prince's Hall (where his only son Juan was born) and with the Bedroom of the Moorish Kings, all chambers with fine decoration.

In the so called **Halls of Charles V (Salones de Carlos V)**, in the other side of the premises, next to the Patio of the Crossing (Patio del Crucero), are shown a considerable collection of Flemish tapestries. In these halls was celebrated, in 1526, the marriage of the emperor with Isabella of Portugal.

And we still have the exquisite **gar-**

GARDENS OF THE ROYAL FORTRESSES.

LABYRINTH OF THE MYRTLE.

POND OF MERCURY.

dens, that constitute an excellent sample of an art in which the Andalusian are great masters. Along the centuries the gardens saw their artistical heritage grow with pavilions, fountains, statues, and even with a labyrinth. Stands out the big pond with the figure of Mercury, the Garden of the Dance (Jardín de la Danza), the adjoined baths of Doña María de Padilla, the Gardens of the Prince, or the cute Pavilion of Charles V, that keeps one of the best cofferings of the fortress. In one of the ends of the garden's premises is the Door of Marchena, from the 16th century, which comes from a palace of the city. The halt, a hall with marble columns from the 18th century, has carriages from that period. Next to it opens the **Patio de Banderas (Patio of Flags)**, a broad space like a parade ground of the Fortress and which also links with the Santa Cruz quarters. It receives this name for the flags that were exposed there when some king lived in the palace.

DOOR OF
MARCHENA.

THREE ASPECTS OF THE SANTA CRUZ QUARTERS AND JUDERÍA STREET.

The first thing one observes when arriving to Seville is that the city seems to be wrapped up in a enchanting and scented bright atmosphere. The light and the flowers are two elements which are closely molten with the spirit of Seville. This is not a well-tryed cliché, it's something that one can realize in any place of the city and specially in the delicious quarters of Santa Cruz, which is, together with Triana, one of the most popular and beloved quarters of the Sevillians. All here is of careful cleanliness and heady perfume. The streets, peaceful and narrow, are flanked with delightful houses with their white fa-

Judería Street.

VENERABLES SQUARE.

GLORIA STREET. ▶

cades partially covered by the greenness of the ivy and the green and white of the jasmines, which impregnate the air with their pleasant scent. With no doubt, getting lost in the enchanted labyrinth of streets and squares of the Santa Cruz quarters represents a remarkable pleasure.

There are also artistical, historical and purely anecdotal elements that contribute to bring out the intrinsic interest of the quarters, like the fact that in an ignored point of the Santa Cruz Square are buried the rests of Murillo, or that in the old Hospital of the Venerable

Priests (Hospital de los Venerables Sacerdotes) you can admire a splendid Baroque patio, or the possible evocation of the legend of the Jewish Susona, whose love towards a young Christian man made her commit treason against her own father and apostatize her faith, receiving as a reward the abandonment of the beau, and who stipulated in her testament that, as expiation, once dead, her head should be placed on top of the door of her house, where, apparently, her skull stayed until the 18th century. A glazed tile in the Susona Street recalls today this story.

The quarters keeps the fundamental layout of what used to be the old quarters of the Jewish community of Seville, where these settled, after the expulsion of the Moorish. From the 16th century onwards the quarters acquire its present appearance after the opening of new squares and the enlargement of streets. In the 19th century the style of the quarter consolidates with the placing of the wrought iron gates which allow to admire the internal patios from the street. When walking in the quarters, one discovers suggestive corners at each step.

HOSPITAL OF THE VENERABLE PRIESTS.

In the **Street of the Jewish Quarters (calle de la Judería)**, next to the fortress, two columns are distinguished which are joined by a chain. The popular saying says that "nobody who wants to get married should jump over them". The street of the Jewish Quarters connects with the **Water Alley (callejón del Agua)**, parallel to the walls of the fortress and called so for the water that in days gone by used to run by the wall. In this last street lived, in number 2, Washington Irving, author of *Tales of Alhambra* (1832).

CERRAJERÍA CROSS.

In the romantic **Square of Doña Elvira (Plaza de Doña Elvira)** existed the famous open-air Theater of Comedies where the Sevillian dramatist Lope de Rueda (1500-1565) started his career. The **Hospital of the Venerable Priests (Hospital de los Venerables Sacerdotes)**, in the square that is named after it, nowadays headquarters of the cultural foundation Focus, is one of the most notable Baroque palaces of Seville. It was built between 1675 and 1695 by a design of Leonardo Figueroa and decorated with painting of Valdés Leal and his son Lucas Valdés.

In the Santa Teresa street, in number 8, is the **House of Murillo (Casa de Murillo)**, where the famous Sevillian painter lived his last years and died. Also in this street is the **Convent of San Jose**, from the 17th century, where relics of Santa Teresa are kept.

In the Square of Santa Cruz, created during the French domination after the knock down of the Santa Cruz church, where Murillo was buried and where before was situated a synagogue, we can admire the **Cross of the Locksmiths (Cruz de Cerrajería)**, an original iron filigree forged in 1692. In the

Refiner's Square (Plaza de los Refinadores) stands out the statue of one of the most biggest myths of Seville, don Juan Tenorio.

To finish we have to mention the **Murillo Gardens (Jardines de Murillo)**, that open to the South of the quarters. It was the old vegetable garden of the Royal Fortress which in 1911 was donated to the city. The gardens were designed by Juan Talavera, also author, together with Collaut Valera, of the monument to Columbus. This monument is composed of two columns with an image of the Santa Maria caravel and, in its cornice, a figure of a lion.

MURILLO GARDENS AND REFINADORES SQUARE.

BRIDGE OF ISABEL II OR OF TRIANA.   BRIDGE OF THE FIFTH CENTENNIAL AND BRIDGE OF CHAPINA. ▶

The Betis is a river with much history. At its banks flowered the prodigious Tartessian civilization. Later it gave name to the Bética, valued rosette of the Roman power, it witnessed the Moorish invasion (who gave it the present denomination) and also the liberating arrival of the troops of Ferdinand III the Saint, it received the ships that came back to Spain after the discovery of America and it saw Magellan and Elcano part to pursuit new discoveries. The Betis is, in resumé, the natural channel of the Sevillian history and the vital artery of the city.

In the Arenal, area that goes from the bullfighting ring of the Real Maestranza to the Santander Street, where the naval dockyards from where the ships departed and arrived to and from the New Continent were, there also were Customs and the House of Mint (Casa de la Moneda). In the other side of the river is the quarter of Triana and the Isle of la Cartuja. At the middle of the 20th century, due to the constant rising of its waters, an embankment was built and part of the course of the stream that crossed the city was diverted. Nowadays, the boats that cleave its waters are mainly touristic, a revealing excursion that allows to get a different view of Seville. The jetty of these boats is next to the Tower of the Gold (Torre del Oro). Many bridges cross the Guadalquivir. The eldest is the one called of **Elizabeth II (Isabel II)**, more known as of Triana, opened in 1852 to replace a previous one called of the Boats (de las Barcas), until then the only communications point between the two banks. The **bridge of San Telmo**, next to the Torre del Oro, was built between 1925 and 1931 and until 1960 it had a central platform that could be raised and lowered to let the big ships pass through. The **bridge of Alfonso XIII**, at the end of the Delights Avenue (Paseo de las Delicias), is dated from 1926. Last to mention the five bridges of innovating design raised as a result of the Universal Exhibition in 1992: from South to North they are the **bridge of the Fifth Centennial** (raised to 43 m of height, being the biggest one), bridge of **Chapina**, bridge of **Cartuja**, bridge of **Barqueta** and of **Alamillo**.

BRIDGE OF
BARQUETA.

BRIDGE OF
ALAMILLO.

TOWER OF THE GOLD.

The **Tower of the Gold (Torre del Oro)**, presently another of the most emblematic monuments of Seville, was built by the almohades at the beginning of the 13th century to control the flow of the river Gualdalquivir, since it was connected to another similar tower at the opposite bank of the river. In the past, it seems, it was covered with golden tiles, from there the name, although the name could also refer to the treasures that arrived from the New World that the ships unloaded next to it.

The tower has a floor of twelve sides and two bodies, the first one done in stone and the second one, of hexagonal floor, of bricks. The cornice was added in 1760. Nowadays, the tower houses an interesting **Naval Museum**, whose contents evoke the history of Seville as a fluvial harbour.

In the past, the Torre del Oro was connected to the walls that Seville defended from the South, which extended up to the Royal Fortress'. Between both points two other towers were raised, nowadays partially hidden between subsequent constructions. One is the **Tower of the Silver (Torre de la Plata)**, in the Santander street next to the Temprado street, of octagonal floor and also from the 13th century, which according to the legend was the place where the keys of the city were given to San Fernando. The other one,

in the Santander street in the corner of the Constitution Avenue, is the **Tower of Abdelaziz**, whose name recalls an old emir of Seville.

From this wall that closed Seville from the South, the Arenal, which was a quarter of shipyards and warehouses, included the area next to the river up to, going North, the Adriano street, and going East, up to the Constitution Avenue. Of the primitive dockyards of Seville today nothing is left, as in the major part of its land were built, at the end of the 16th century, two new buildings, the **House of Mint (Casa de la Moneda)** and **Customs (Aduana)**. In the first one, located in the Santander street in the corner with Maese Rodri-

59

TOWER OF THE SILVER.

go street, is nowadays the **Numismatic Museum**, whose contents include instruments and designs used throughout times to mint coins. The building of Customs, in the adjoining street of Tomás de Ibarra, was totally rebuilt in 1795 due to a fire and which is nowadays headquarters of the Local Tax Office. At the end of Tomás de Ibarra street is located the **Shutter of the Oil (Postigo del Aceite)**, an old door of access to the city which the Almoravides opened in the 12th century, although it was totally reformed in 1573. The name recalls the importance of the oil business in Seville, already since the Roman period. In one of its sides, in the wall, there is a small chapel that keeps the image of the Pure and Clean Conception of the Holy Virgin Maria (Pura y Limpia Concepción de María Santísima). And just beside it, the Seises Passage takes you to the **Cabildo Square**, a beautiful square with columns where takes place, on Sundays, a small street market dedicated to philately and numismatics.

Other interesting places in the Arenal are the Hospital of Charity and the Bullfighting Ring of the Real Maestranza, which will be dealt in separate chapters, the Theater of the Maestranza and the chapels of Carretería and of Baratillo.

The **Theater of the Maestranza**, in Cristopher Columbus Avenue, was opened in 1991 and it is designed by Aurelio del Pozo and Luis Marín de Terán, who kept in the main facade the big front railings of the Artillery Park and Armory (Parque y Maestranza de Artillería), a munitions factory of the 19th century that existed in this place. Of circular floor, it was conceived specially as an opera theater, its program, how-

POSTIGO DEL ACEITE.

THEATER OF THE MAESTRANZA.

ever, includes all kinds of cultural events. It also is the headquarters of the Symphony Orchestra of Seville. It has a capacity of audience for 1,800 persons. The **chapel of Carretería**, in the Varflora street, was founded by the guild of barrel makers and cart drivers and it worships the images of the Christ of the Health (Cristo de la Salud) and Our Lady of the Main Suffering (Nuestra Señora del Mayor Dolor). The **chapel of Baratillo** is in the Adriano street and it keeps the images of Our Lady of Pity (Nuestra Señora de la Piedad) and of the Christ of Mercy (Cristo de la Misericordia), which comes out, this last one, in procession during the Holy Week.

CABILDO SQUARE.

PATIO OF THE HOSPITAL OF THE CHARITY.

This institution, which still works as an old people's home, is one of the most privileged artistical places of Seville, since it has a magnificent art gallery with masterpieces of Valdés Leal and Murillo concerning themes such as death and compassion. Don Miguel de Mañara (1627-1679), who totally was dedicated to this institution after living a dissolute life, was its main beneficent and he stipulated the iconographic program which has given good reputation to the place, with what he intended to transmit was the message that the Christian only can achieve the eternal sal-

vation through charity. A monument dedicated to this aristocrat, done by the Sevillian sculptor Antonio Susillo, can be admired outside, in front of the building, whereas his rests lie in the crypt of the church. In the gravestone of the tomb where don Miguel was initially buried, in the atrium, appeared this epitaph written by Mañara himself: "Here lie the bones and the ashes of the worst man that lived in this world". From here possibly starts the origin of the false legend of don Miguel de Mañara, to whom the Romantic authors wanted to identify with the Don Juan created by Tirso de Molina in his book

The Seducer of Seville (*El Burlador de Sevilla*). According to other theories, Mañara founded the hospital after the crisis he suffered as a consequence of the death of his young and beloved wife.

The building of the Hospital is organized around a big double patio, divided in two spaces with a high passage on top of columns, drawn by Leonardo de Figueroa in 1682. In each one of these spaces there is a marble fountain with a group of sculptures that represent Mercy and Charity. The mentioned patio connects with three rooms that were built using the space of old

Gothic naves of the antique dockyards of Seville, and with the church, dedicated to San Jorge.

It is in the church where are kept the famous painting of Valdés Leal and Murillo, this last one a very close friend of Mañara. Next to the entrance, under the choir, are placed the entitled *In ictu oculi* (in a twinkling of an eye) and *Finis gloriae mundi* (the end of the earthly glories), two masterpieces of Juan Valdés Leal done in 1671 and 1672,

of moving reality. It is said that Murillo, when he contemplated the second one said: "Compare, to see this you have to hold your nose". The iconographic program continued with four paintings of Murillo which were taken away by marshal Soult during the Independence War, later replaced by four passages of the Bible, and ends up with the paintings, also by Murillo, of *The miracle of the multiplication of the breads, The miracle of the waters*

of Moses and, in the main retable, *Compassion*.

There are more painting of Murillo in the temple, of which we can *mention Saint John of God carrying an ill person*, where the portrait of the Saint is identified with don Miguel de Mañara, *and Saint Elizabeth of Hungary healing the mangy*. To finish, we have to mention the magnificent main retable, which contains one of the best sculptures of Pedro Roldán, *The funeral of Christ*, done between 1670 and 1674.

MIGUEL DE MAÑARA MONUMENT.

HOSPITAL OF THE CHARITY: FACADE OF THE CHURCH.

AERIAL VIEW OF THE BULLFIGHTING RING OF THE REAL MAESTRANZA.

The famous bullfighting ring of the Real Maestranza is, without no doubt, one of the most prestigious places of tauromachy. It was built in the 18th century and restored in the middle of the 19th century. The imposing architectonic presence of the Sevillian bullfighting ring harmonized perfectly with its history and its prestige. It is spacious, comfortable and beautiful as few, and it represents an ideal setting to, on the sand of the ring, carry out the ritual of the bullfight. The taurine record of Seville is so antique as distinguished. Not only have passed through the Maestranza the most famous bullfighters of all periods, but in the city have born many of the biggest figures of the tauromachy, such as Pepe-Hillo (creator of the verónica), El Espartero, Belmonte, Gitanillo de Triana, Rafael el Gallo, Cagancho, Chicuelo, the great Joselito (whose rests lie in the Sevillian cemetery of San Fernando, in an artistical pantheon sculpt by Mariano Benlliure) and many other famous swords. On the other hand, Seville has a long bull breeding tradition, backed up by names like Miura, Pablo Romero, Murube or Saltillo.

In the taurine calendar of Seville are underlined the bullfights of the April Fair, of Easter Sunday and of the festivity of Corpus Christi. The bullfighting ring has a capacity for 12,500 spectators. The main entrance, called Door of the Prince (Puerta del Príncipe), opens to the Cristopher Columbus Avenue. It is from this door from where the bullfighters that have triumphed are carried out on shoulders. Behind the entrance is the Main Box or of the Prince, reserved to the Royal Family. Philip V decided that the "big brother" of the Real Maestranza de Caballería, institution which is the owner of the bullfighting ring, would be a member of the royal family. For this reason the Box of the Prince was created, and it remains closed when no member of the royal family is present.

In adjoining premises is the **Taurine Museum**, which keeps historical remembrances of this bullfighting ring, as well as a cape painted by Picasso. In an adjoining building are located the library and the House and Chapel of the Real Maestranza de Caballería. The guided tour includes a visit to the infirmary and the patios where the horses of the 'picadores' are.

MAIN FACADE OF THE FINE ARTS MUSEUM.

Installed in the old convent of the Merced Calzada, in the number 9 of the Museum Square. The building was finished in 1612, under the management of the architect Juan de Oviedo, but in 1810, due to a fire, it had to be restored completely. Later it was restored in many other occasions, already as headquarters of the museum, to improve the installations. The building is organized around three patios that are decorated with tiles and full of flowers and trees. The church, also converted in to a exhibitions hall, preserves a magnificent dome painted by Domingo Martínez in the 18th century.

The initial pictorical background of the museum comes from the forced ex-monastic status produced as consequence of the confiscation of the clergy's properties ordered in 1836. Four years later the Museum of Fine Arts settled in the abandoned convent. As a whole, for the category and quantity of its contents it is considered the most important Spanish art gallery after the Museum of Prado.

The museum counts with a valuable and copious collection of paintings from the Sevillian School from the 15th and 16th centuries. It is also considerable the group of paintings of the most famous Spanish painters from the 17th century, like Valdés

"Portrait of elderly people",
of Francisco Pacheco.

Leal, Murillo, Zurbarán, Alonso Cano, Francisco Pacheco and Herrera. El Greco is represented by a marvellous oil painting with the portrait of his son Jorge Manuel, and we have to add also several paintings of Velázquez and of foreign artists like Bosch, Rubens, Veronés and Tiziano. Besides, the museum also exposes sculptures, ivories, works of ceramics and furniture.

"Brother Hortensio de Paravicino", of El Greco.
"Imposition of the chasuble to San Idelfonso", of Velázquez.

"BAPTISM OF SAN JERÓNIMO", OF VALDÉS LEAL.　　　HALL WITH WORKS OF MURILLO INSTALLED IN THE OLD CHURCH. ▶

The best represented painters are Zurbarán, Murillo and Juan de Valdés Leal. Of Zurbarán there are more than twenty paintings, among which outstand *The Virgin of the Caves, Apotheosis of Saint Thomas of Aquino, Pope Urban II, Saint Huge in the refectory* and *Saint Luis Beltrán.* Of Murillo, the museum counts with the best collection of this Sevillian artist, among them *The Virgin Purísima, The Virgin of the Serviette, Saints Justa and Rufina, Saint*

PORTRAIT OF ISABEL II, OF ANTONIO MARÍA ESQUIVEL.

Joseph, The Blessed Virgin Girl and *Saint Antonio de Padua*. From Valdés Leal, from who there are more than twenty paintings, stand out the paintings *The defeat of the Saracen in front of the walls of Asis, The temptations of Saint Jeronimo, The Mass of Father Cabañuelas* and *Saint Clare with the Monstrance*.

You can also admire excellent paintings of Pantoja de la Cruz, Pacheco, Herrera the Old, El Bosco, El Españoleto, Van Dyck, Roelas, Correggio, Rubens, Tiziano, Veronés, Claudio de Lorena, Poussin and, of Goya, the portrait of don José Pinazo.

Among the painters of the 19th century, the best represented is the Sevillian Esquivel, who, with his excellent gallery of portraits of ladies and gentlemen, offers a valid social image of the Elizabethan period. From that century you can also admire paintings of Gonzalo de Bilbao – like his exceptional *The Cigar Sellers*, Madrazo, Valeriano Domínguez Bécquer, Martínez Cubells, Jiménez Aranda and Muñoz Degrain. The sculptural work is also of great importance, standing out some sculptures by an anonymous author and others of Sedano, Torrigiano, Martínez Montañés, Juan de Mesa, Pedro de Mena and Luisa Roldán.

"SUMMER NIGHT IN SEVILLE", OF GONZALO DE BILBAO.

SAN FRANCISCO SQUARE: CITY HALL.

The City Hall of Seville is located between the historical San Francisco Square and the **New Square (plaza Nueva)**. This last one is one of the most pleasant of the city, full of palm trees and with banks to rest. In the middle of this square is an equestrian monument of San Fernando and, partially hidden between the modern buildings, is the **chapel of Saint Onofre**, only remain of the convent of San Francisco, which until the middle of the 19th century occupied this whole place. The **San Francisco square** carries out since a very long time the function of main center of the city. Its present structure, nevertheless, responds to a reform done in the first half of the 16th century, period in which the building of the City Hall was

raised, the fountain with the sculpture of God Mercury, the old Royal Prison (Cárcel Real), situated at the beginning of the Sierpes street, and the palace of the Royal Court (Audiencia Real), today headquarters of a Savings Bank. The square was during the Middle Age a business center, scene of tournaments and bullfightings and of public executions at the time of the Inquisition, as well as a privileged place in Easter, while here are installed the boxes to watch the procession of all the brotherhoods and the monstrance of Arfe on Corpus Christi's day.

The **City Hall (Ayuntamiento)** was built between 1527 and 1534 under the management of Diego de Riaño, also master builder of the cathedral, who conceived a great building to high-

light the grandeur of the emerging city of Seville. It is one of the most historical Renaissance architecture buildings of Spain, although the facade which opens to the New Square dates from the 19th century. In one of its sides, the popular "Arquillo" served as access to the disappeared convent of San Francisco. In there are the sculptured figures of Hercules and Julius Caesar, the legendary founders of the city.

Inside stand out in the lobby, the Chapterhouse (Sala Capitular), old headquarters of the famous Twentyfive Gentlemen of the City, whose stone dome is almost flat and is decorated with 36 artistical coffer mouldings that represent the figures of the Spanish kings till Charles V, the magnificent staircase that goes to the Historical Archive

CHAPEL OF SAN JOSÉ.

SIERPES STREET.

and the beautiful Columbus Hall (Salón de Colón). In the Archive are kept documents of great historical value related to Alfonso X, Peter I, the Catholic Monarchs, Philip II and other monarchs, and autographs of Miguel de Mañara, Cervantes, Herrera the Divine and Alonso Cano, among others. The art gallery of the city hall is very important and it is composed of works by Valdés Leal, Zurbarán and other renown masters. It is also interesting the collection of jewellery and antique objects, among which stand out the Banner of the City, from the mid 15th century.

In the San Francisco square begins the famous and busy **Sierpes street**. Its bars and terraces have been a traditional meeting point for the Sevillians and a coming and going area during all times. To scour it and participate of it is another way to know Seville and its people. Just in the entrance of the street was the mentioned Royal Prison, where Miguel de Cervantes was imprisoned and it is even said that it was there where he wrote his immortal *Don Quixote de la Mancha*. A bit further, in the adjoining street of Jovellanos, is the **Chapel of San José**, very small

but of exuberant and extreme Baroque style. Between the Rivero and Azofaifo streets rise the walls of the **Palace of the Countess of Lebrija**, whose main entrance is located in the Cuna street. Built in the 15th and 16th centuries, it is one of the best samples of a Sevillian palace and it contains, besides, several Roman pieces, to stand out the mosaic floor of the main patio, of which the great majority come from the ruins of Italica. At last, we have to mention, that at the end of the Sierpes street is La Campana, the most famous cake shop of the city.

MAIN PATIO OF THE PALACE OF THE COUNTESS OF LEBRIJA. ▶

SETAS DE LA ENCARNACIÓN.

The Metropol Parasol, an original architectural structure in Plaza de la Encarnación that is popularly known as **Las Setas de la Encarnación** ("The Mushrooms of the Incarnation), due to its resemblance to a crop of mushrooms, officially opened in March 2011. The structure provides shelter from the sun, but visitors can also go up to the top of it to obtain interesting views over the city. The site measures 70 x 150 metres and is 26 metres in height. The forms and materials used by the Berlin architect Jürgen Mayer-Hermann, who designed the structure, are in stark contrast to the surrounding environment, for this "parasol" is a truly striking creation. Besides the viewpoint, the site also accommodates a market (on ground level), a restaurant and a plaza for shows (on the middle level) and the Antiquarium Museum (underground). The area was previously occupied by a market, but this was demolished in 1973 due to its ruinous state. When construction of a new car park began in the 1990s, important archaeological remains were found, and work was halted. A public competition was launched for the rehabilitation of the square, showcasing this archaeological treasure and restoring it as a market-place. The **Antiquarium Museum** provides the ancient note in this ultra-modern development. Here, the exhibits include a 1st-century saltfish factory, conserved *in situ*, mosaics from Roman houses from the 2nd to the 5th century and the remains of dwellings from the Visigoth and Almohad periods.

Several ancient monuments in the city have also been converted into

ANTIGUA REAL AUDIENCIA.

museums and cultural centres. One such is the former palace of justice, or **Antigua Real Audiencia**, in Plaza de San Francisco, near the Town Hall. The building dates to the late-16th century, though the façade was completely reformed in 1926. Now the headquarters of a bank, the site houses an important collection of painting from all periods in art history, including a Murillo, as well as sculptures and furniture. At the **Museum of the Castle of San Jorge**, in Triana,

beside the market, visitors can view what was, from the 15th to the 18th century, the feared Court of the Holy Inquisition in Seville. The site is now designed to foster thought and meditation. Finally, on a lighter note, the **Torre de los Perdigones** is installed with a camera obscura. This tower, 45 metres high, stands in Calle Resolana, near the river. Built in 1890, it originally formed part of a factory making lead shot ("perdigones" in Spanish).

TORRE DE LOS PERDIGONES.

SALVADOR'S CHURCH.

The **Salvador church**, in the square of the same name, is a clear exponent of the splendour of the Baroque period in Seville. It was built between 1671 and 1712 on top of the Ibn Addabas mosque, which was the main mosque of Seville until the Almohade was raised in the place of the cathedral. After the Christian conquest, the mosque was converted in to a collegiate church and later, due to its bad state, the construction of the present building was decided. Of the primitive Muslim temple only part of the patio of ablutions was preserved, while the minaret was finished off with a body of Baroque bells.

Various architects participated in the construction. Esteban García was the first master builder and Leonardo de Figueroa who finished the temple. Stand out the huge main retable and the one of the sacramental chapel, both done by Cayetano Acosta. The images the church contains are also of great value, to mention the image of *The Most Holy Christ of Love* by Juan de Mesa and the image of *Jesus of the Passion*

SAN ILDEFONSO'S CHURCH.

and *Saint Cristobal* by Juan Martínez Montañés, of whom stands out today a monument at the Salvador square.

In this same square is the **church and hospital of San Juan de Dios**, more known as of Our Lady of the Peace (Nuestra Señora de la Paz). The hospital dates from the ends of the 16th century and the church is subsequent, from the 17th century. In there stand out the tiles that decore the side walls, the plaster works of the choir's gallery and the grille of the pulpit.

The **church of Saint Isidoro**, in the Luchana street, is of Mudejar trace. It was built in the 14th century and in there stands out, inside, a sculpture of Simón Cirineo done by Antonio Francisco Gijón in 1687.

The **church of Saint Ildefonso**, in the square of the same name, presents a facade of lively colours and two high neoclassical towers. It keeps two interesting sculptures of the great Sevillian religious image maker Pedro Roldán, *Saint Hermenegildo* and *Saint Ferdinand*.

The **convent of Saint Leandro**, in the Caballerizas street, is above all known for its delicious sweets made of egg yolk and sugar called 'yemas de San Leandro'. The convent is dated from the 13th century, but the church was not raised until the 17th century. The main altar represents another good sample of the Sevillian Baroque style.

Finally, we have to mention the **Minor Basilica of Our Father Jesus of the Great Power**, which houses this brotherhood, in the San Lorenzo square. It is a modern construction, of 1965, and its main interesting feature is the image of Jesus of the Great Power, known also as the "Lord of Seville", which is one of the most worshiped images of the city, a work by Juan de Mesa of 1620. A visit to its museum allows to know, besides, the procession equipment of this brotherhood.

MINOR BASILICA OF OUR FATHER JESUS OF THE GREAT POWER.

ALAMEDA DE HÉRCULES BOULEVARD AND SAN PEDRO'S CHURCH.

The Macarena is one of the traditional quarters of Seville that, together with Triana, has best known how to preserve its identity marks. It expands towards North, starting from the Laraña street or the San Pedro square and up to the area of the walls of the Macarena. There exists various hypothesis about the origin of the name. For some it is of Roman origin and comes from *Macariusena* (property of Macario) or from the goddess Macaria, daughter of Hercules. Other say that the name comes from the palaces of a Moorish princess. The **Feria street** is the main artery of the quar-

ters. In this street and in the adjoining Amargura street every Thursday is settled, since the Medieval period, a popular street market where it is possible to find anything. At night, the **Alameda de Hércules** is full of life, revolving around the bars and restaurants here. Presiding over these pleasant gardens, which have stood here since the late-16th century, are two columns bearing the statues of Hercules and Julius Caesar respectively.

Among the several churches and convents of the quarters we have to mention the **church of Saint Pedro** and the **convent of Saint Inés**, both of

Gothic-Mudejar trace, although with many later alterations; the first one is also known because Velázquez received his baptism there in 1599; the **church of Saint Catalina**, built in the 14th century on top of a mosque of which is preserved the niche of the mihrab and the minaret; the **convent of Saint Paula**, of the 15th century, keeps sculptures by Martínez Montañés and a magnificent collection of paintings and gold articles; the **church of Saint Marcos**, from the 15th century, whose tower reminds the Giralda; the **convent of Saint Clara**, from the 15th century, in whose patio is the **Tower**

SANTA CATALINA'S CHURCH.

of Don Fabrique, from the 13th century, unique remain of the old palace of the infante don Fadrique and to which we recommend to climb for the fantastic views you can see of the city. The **monastery of Saint Clemente**, founded by Alfonso X and which belongs to the Cistercian order, and which has one of the best Mudejar cofferings of Seville, as well as frescos done by Valdés Leal and notable tiles, and finally, for its significance for the Sevillians, the **basilica of the Macarena**. The worshiped image of the Virgin Hope Macarena (Virgen Esperanza Macarena) was kept in the adjoining church of Saint Gil, from the 13th century, until it suffered a fire in 1936. It was then decided the construction of a new building, which was raised between 1941 and 1946 according to a project of Aurelio Gómez Millán in neobaroque style and which is a basilica since 1966. The image, in the main altar, is adorned with a great amount of gold and silver. The author is unknown, although it is attributed to Luisa Roldán "La Roldana". In the early hours of Good Friday, when

CHURCH OF SAINT MARCOS AND TOWER OF DON FABRIQUE.

the image is taken out in procession, the square converts in to the scene of the greatest popular fervour. To the cry of 'Guapa!' (Beautiful!), the path of the Virgin of Macarena crosses the city to the Cathedral. In the museum, situated in the Treasure hall, are exposed the different equipments of this popular Brotherhood, founded in 1595 and which did its first station of penance in 1624. Stand out the rich cloaks and jewellery of the Virgin and several bullfighter's costumes given by famous bullfighters. Other interesting sculptures which are found in the basilica are the Virgin Rosario, from the 18th century and attributed to Pedro Duque Cornejo, and the figure of the Christ of the Judgement (Cristo de la Sentencia), work done by Felipe Morales Nieto in 1654.

Next to the basilica, the so called **Arch of Macarena** corresponds to the old door of "Bab-al-Markina" from the Almoravid period, which was completely reformed in the 19th century. Following the arch we find the unique section which is preserved of the **walls** that surrounded the city, which extends on until the **church of Saint Hermenegildo**, next to the Capuchinos road. This chapel,

BASÍLICA OF MACARENA. HOLY WEEK: RETURN OF THE VIRGIN TO HER TEMPLE.

ANDALUSIAN PARLIAMENT.

PALACE OF DUEÑAS.

which was raised in the place where according to the legend suffered martyrdom this saint Visigothic king in 578, it incorporates the **Door of Cordoba** in its walls, a typical Moorish door of horseshoe arch. The tradition says that from this door entered Ferdinand III dressed up as a Muslim to inspect the city before conquering it. The old walls were demolished in the mid 19th century, except this section that was decided to keep as a memory of those times.

On the other side of the walls, in front of the basilica of Macarena, is the enormous Renaissance building of the old Hospital of the Blood, also known as of the Five Wounds, which since 1992 is the head office of the **Parliament of Andalusia**. The building has four patios and it preserves the church, work of Hernán Ruiz from 1560 in mannerism style, which is used nowadays as a debate hall.

Before leaving the quarters, we have to mention the **Palace of Dueñas**, in the street of the same name, a beautiful exponent of a Sevillian palace house. Built in the 15th century, its architecture combines the Mudejar, Gothic and Plateresque styles. In the main entrance stands out a shield from the 18th century. The beautiful garden that follows was originally a space used as an exercise ring and stable for horses. But above all stands out the main patio, decorated with Gothic plaster works and a Plateresque balustrade. The palace belonged to the Dukes of Montijo and there were born the poets Antonio and Manuel Machado, sons of a highly con-

sidered employee of the duke. Nowadays it is property of the Dukes of Alba and you have to previously request in writing permission to visit it.

MAIN PATIO OF THE HOUSE OF PILATE.

In the Pilate square is located this exquisite palace, which is the most splendid of Seville after the Royal Fortress'. The order to build it was done by Pedro Enríquez, head governor of Andalusia, but its highest sponsor was his son Don Fadrique after returning from his trip to the Holy Land in 1519. The general idea that he was raising a copy of the praetory of the procurator of Judea Pontius Pilate gave origin to its name. Others attribute the name to the fact that it was the first station of a Via Crucis (Jesus facing Pilate) which started here and finished in the Cross of Campo, at the outskirts of the city.

Nowadays it belongs to the Dukes of Medinaceli.

In love with the marvels that he had seen in Jerusalem, and specially in Italy, but also a great admirer of the Mudejar art, Don Fadrique created in this palace a whole of extraordinary interest for its wise combination of styles.

The main facade, looking like a Roman triumphal arch, was done in Genova in 1529. In continuation, a portico connects with the horse stables and the splendid main patio. This patio presents marble columns which support irregular arches decorated with elaborated Mudejar plaster works and

crowned with Gothic balustrade; the central fountain, of Renaissance style, was imported from Genova, the baseboards are covered with tiles from the 16th century and in the friezes are shown 24 busts of Roman emperors and of other figures of the Classical times; in the four corners are two sculptures of the goddess Athenea (one of them is a copy of the original Greek one sculpt by Phidia in the 5th century BC), another one of the goddess Ceres and the fourth one corresponds to a dancing Muse.

To the right of the main patio are the Golden Hall and the Praetory Hall, with a splendid Mudejar coffering. From a

THE GREAT
GARDEN.

PRAETORY HALL AND MAIN STAIRCASE.

corridor where are exposed several archaeological pieces (to highlight the bas-relief *Leda and the swan*) you pass to the Small Garden, with a decorated pond with Roman and Renaissance statues.

You have to go back to the main patio to visit the rest of the rooms of the ground floor: The hall called Rest of the Judges, with a tile baseboard and frieze of plaster work, the small chapel called of the Flagellation –a combination of Gothic and Mudejar styles– which keeps a sculpture of the 4th century, *The Good Shepherd* and the Cabinet of Pilate essentially Mudejar, from which you can reach the Great Gar-

den, of Italian style, closed in three fronts by loggia done by the Italian architect Benvenutto Tortello in 1560 (one of them conditioned as house of the Dukes of Medinaceli) and with classical statues from the 16th century.

You get to the upper floor, from the main patio, through a monumental staircase of four flights, whose original design converts it in one the most exceptional ones of Spain. It is profusely decorated with colourful tiles and covered by a dome of bows with Arab scallops done in 1537 by Cristóbal Sánchez and Antón Pérez. The top halls keep an excellent art gallery, as well as sculptures and furniture.

Seville is, along with Jerez de la Frontera (Cádiz province), the cradle of Flamenco art, singing and dancing. The roots of Flamenco go back to the Middle Ages, when Gypsies mixed Moorish and Andalusian folklore with Jewish and Christian music in their songs and dances. Nonetheless, it was not until the 18th century that the forms we know today began to emerge. In the Andalusian capital, *sevillanas* are the most popular Flamenco dances, and these and many other dances, as well as guitar, *cante* and *palmas*, are regularly performed by outstanding artists at Flamenco *tablaos* all over the city. These shows are found particularly in two neighbourhoods, Santa Cruz and Triana, though fans visit the latter particularly to hear *cante jondo*, for Triana is the cradle of great *cantaores*. Apart from the April Fair, one of the great events in the calendar for Flamenco lovers is the **Biennial of Flamenco Art** (September and October).

Opened in 2006 in Calle Manuel Rojas Marcos, five minutes' walk from the Cathedral, the **Museum of Flamenco Dance** is devoted to exploring the essence of this art. Conceived as an "experience museum", this centre not only illustrates the history and present situation of Flamenco, but also enables visitors to experience the feelings that this art can awaken, by hearing the different *palos*, sharing the joy transmitted by Flamenco dance, understanding the hard work and sacrifice that professional *bailaores* and *bailaoras* must make, seeing the pain that Flamenco expresses and, in short, thrilling to the power of this form of artistic expression.

MUSEUM OF FLAMENCO DANCE: FAÇADE, PROJECTION ROOM AND PATIO (COURTYARD).
PHOTOGRAPHS: © MUSEO DEL BAILE FLAMENCO.

FOUNTAIN IN THE PUERTA DE JEREZ SQUARE, AND THE HOTEL ALFONSO XIII.

The **Door of Jerez** was the exit from the length of wall towards the grounds of the wine, Jerez de la Frontera and Cádiz. Knocked down in 1864, since the beginnings of the 20th century its place is occupied by a slender fountain, work of Delgado Brackenbury. This square is surrounded by distinguished buildings the **Palace of Yanduri**, of French style, from the 20th century; the **chapel of Master Rodrigo**, a small Gothic-Mudejar temple which is the only remain of the primitive University of Seville, founded by Master Rodrigo in 1502 and demolished with the extension works at the beginnings of the 20th century of the Constitution Avenue, and which keeps beautiful tiles and a notable retable of

the painter Alejo Fernández; the so called **House of the Guardiola**, a reminiscent of the Renaissance style, and the **Hotel Alfonso XIII**, the most luxurious one of Seville, which was built between 1916 and 1928 in a neo-mudejar style for the Latin American Exhibition of 1929.

Very near of the Hotel Alfonso XIII, in the Avenue of Rome is the **Palace of Saint Telmo**, built at the end of the 17th century, although its facade of churrigueresque style dates from the 18th century and is own to the architect Leonardo de Figueroa. In its beginnings it kept the Navigation School, and so it is remembered by the central figure of the facade, Saint Telmo, patron saint of the navigators, who ap-

pears surrounded by allegorical sculptures related with navigation. When still being a Navy school –it stopped being it in 1848–, Gustavo Adolfo Bécquer studied there.

In 1849 it became the residence of the Duke of Montpensier, pretender to the Spanish throne and the Palace of Saint Telmo was converted during some time in center of antidynastic conspiracies. The splendid gardens of the Park of María Luisa formed part of the palace until 1893, date in which the infanta María Luisa, duchess of Montpensier, already a widow and seeing frustrated her aspirations to the throne, gave them to the city, whereas the palace was given in 1901 to the Archbishopric, which installed here the

Main Seminary. In 1992 the building was bought and restored by the Junta of Andalusia to house the headquarters of the Junta's presidency.

Apart from the main facade is of interest the facade that gives to the Avenue of Palos de la Frontera, in whose frieze are represented twelve famous Sevillians, among which we can find Murillo, Velázquez and Martínez Montañés, work by Antonio Susillo from 1895. From the inside we have to mention the broad patio, the Hall of the Columns, both from the 18th century, and the chapel, of Baroque style, in whose main altar stands out an image of Our Lady of the Good Air (Nuestra Señora del Buen Aire), to whom is attributed the origin of the name of the capital of Argentina.

Behind the Palace of Saint Telmo and of the Hotel Alfonso XIII is the enormous building (250 x 180 meters) of the **University of Seville**, head office of the Vice-Chancellor and of several Faculties. It was built between 1728 and 1771 to house the Tobacco Factory of Seville, since the primitive factory, located in the center of the city, had become small and obsolete given the magnitude that this activity achieved. Seville enjoyed the monopoly of the production of tobacco, being during a long time one of the most richest industries of Spain and which had the biggest number of workers. It is said that three quarters of the cigars that were smoked in Europe were produced inside its walls.

As it was a public build-

SAN TELMO'S PALACE.

CARMEN MONUMENT, LOCATED IN FRONT OF THE BULLFIGHTING RING.

ing (it depended of the Royal Tax Office) and being a very powerful industry, the grounds were conceived as a citadel. Thus explains the fact that it had a prison, a drawbridge and a moat. It had, besides, a permanent guard to avoid smuggling and the constant black market. Although the building was modified in a later stage for its academic purpose, the two areas in which it was divided can still be appreciated: around the front door was the residential area, while the industry occupied the rest.

The main door, in the San Fernando street, shows an allegory of the Fame and it is decorated with the busts of Cristopher Columbus, discoverer of the world from where the tobacco comes, and of Hernán Cortés, considered the first European who became keen in smoking. After crossing the patios of the Clock and of the Fountain you can reach the old workshops. In them, 116 mills moved by animal traction crumbled the tobacco leaves that previously had been dried at the terrace roofs. The building has not only history, but also literary legend, popularized by Merimée in his novel *Carmen*, a cigar seller who stabs a workmate and later seduces and pushes the sergeant who was in charge of her to start a life of banditry.

On the other hand, the University of Seville was located, since the period of Charles III, in what used to be the Profess House of the Company of Jesus, in whose church in the crypt of are buried the rests of Gustavo Adolfo Bécquer and Arias Montano.

LOPE DE VEGA THEATER.

The most exquisite of the parks of Seville has its origin in the donation done to the city in 1893 by the infanta María Luisa, duchess of Montpensier, of half of the gardens of the Palace of Saint Telmo, which extended to the present square of America. Later, with the celebration of the Latin American Exhibition of 1929, which was held at the same time as the Universal Exhibition of Barcelona, it was decided to arrange all this area, which was extended with the adjoining pieces of land of the Park of San Sebastian (Prado de San Sebastián), the orange trees from the Palace of Saint Telmo, the gardens of the De-lights (next to the river, where the old pavilions of the Exhibition accommodate nowadays consulates and cultural institutions) and the so called Vegetable Garden of Mariana (which today is the America square). The French engineer Forestier was the person in charge to design the gardens and to Aníbal González, first vice-chancellor architect of the Exhibition, we owe great part of the buildings as well as the España and America squares.

What used to be the main entrance of the Exhibition, and today one of the main accesses of the Park of María Luisa, is located at the **Roundabout of Saint Diego (Glorieta de San Diego)**. Of the whole ornamental group that was raised to receive the visitors are left some colonnades and a sculptural group with three feminine figures and a fountain at its base. Before we enter the park you can distinguish behind, in the María Luisa Avenue, the **Lope de Vega Theater**, which was the theater of the Exhibition. The building is of Neobaroque style and it is a work of Vicente Traver, successor of Aníbal González as vice-chancellor architect of the Exhibition.

The Park of María Luisa is a luxuriant garden, specially pleasant against the summer heat, which is layed out in several tree-lined avenues. Next to

PARK OF
MARÍA LUISA.

GUSTAVO ADOLFO BÉCQUER MONUMENT.

the main entrance is the place to rent the traditional horse carriages that make rides in the park, and very near of this entrance is also the **monument to Gustavo Adolfo Bécquer**, surrounding a cypress planted in 1850, done by Lorenzo Collaut Valera of 1912. The figure of the Sevillian poet is accompanied by three women, that symbolize the three states of love –the awaiting, the devotion and the lost–, and two angels, that symbolize the love that wounds and the wounded love. Another outstanding monument of the park is the **Roundabout of the Infanta**, which was raised in honour of the infanta María Luisa of Orleans.

In the central space of the park there is a **pond** with swans and ducks and which has a small island with a romantic pavilion where, according to the legend, Alfonso XII declare his love to María de las Mercedes, and two artistical fountains: the **Fountain of the Frogs**, decorated with ceramics from Triana, and the **Fountain of the Lions**, surrounded by myrtle hedges.

To the left, next to the avenue of Isabel la Católica, opens the spacious

POND OF THE PARK OF MARÍA LUISA.

ESPAÑA SQUARE: AERIAL VIEW AND DETAIL.

España Square, architectural group of singular personality that was conceived by Aníbal González. It is a semicircle of 200 meters of diameter that culminates in two high and stylized towers in its ends. An artificial channel where you can go in a boat passes in its interior, like a division between the great central esplanade and the taller part. Under the balustrades of the colonnades that surround the square are the banks decorated with tiles in which are represented, in alphabetical order, the 54 Spanish provinces. The shield, the provincial

ROYAL PAVILION.

map and regarding symbols to its history identify each one of the provinces. In the arches of the colonnades are inscribed medallions with the busts of famous Spanish figures, from Séneca to Sorolla. At last, the central building presents in its inside a porched patio of two floors, and in the center of the huge esplanade a round fountain offers in the nights spectacular games of water and lights.

The boardness of the square and its special layout produce, when reach-

MUDÉJAR PAVILION, HEADQUARTERS OF THE MUSEUM OF ARTS AND POPULAR CUSTOMS.

PLATERESQUE PAVILION, HEADQUARTERS OF THE ARCHAEOLOGICAL MUSEUM.

ing it after strolling in the shades of the park, a sensation of surprise and dazzle: an tremendous brightness hovers the whole and stands out clearly the smallest details. A similar sensation you get when you arrive to the **America Square**, also designed by Aníbal González. It is a huge space with a fountain in the middle and gardens, surrounded by three buildings which recreate the three historical artistic styles of the city: the Mudejar in the **Mudejar Pavilion**, the Gothic in the **Royal Pavilion** and the Renaissance in the **Plateresque Pavilion**. The Mudejar Pavilion houses, since its

inauguration in 1973, the **Museum of Arts and Popular Customs**. It has an interesting exhibition of ethnographic character, with special emphasis in the decorative arts, the traditional clothes and the objects used in everyday routine, essentially of Seville.

The Plateresque Pavilion is, since 1946, the headquarter of the **Archaeological Museum of Seville**, considered one of the first ones of Spain in its speciality. The main piece of the museum is the called Treasure of Carambolo, a collection of rich jewellery which dates from the Tartessian

culture (6th century BC) and of which the museum shows an exact copy. It was discovered in 1958 in the hill of Carambolo –Camas (Seville)– and it consists of 21 pieces of gold. The pieces are Roman, the majority from Itálica, and they are abundant, but we have to mention the statues of Hermes, Diana, Venus, Trajano and Adriano. Other cultures and people that have forged the history of Andalusia are also represented in the museum and as a testimony of it are several paleochristian sarcophagus, Visigothic items and other rests from the Arab domination period.

PAVILION OF MÉXICO.

The majority of the pavilions that were built for the Exhibition of 1929 are situated in the **Avenue of the Delights (Paseo de las Delicias)** and its continuation called Avenue of the Palmtree (Avenida de la Palmera), which has become in one of the most beautiful arteries of the city. In the most southern stretch is the **Pavilion of Brazil**, work by Pedro Paulo Basto, today head office of the Local Police; the **Pavilion of Mexico**, work by Manuel Amabilis which is inspired in the Maya architecture, the **Pavilion of Colombia**, work by José Granados, today head office of the Navigation School

PAVILION OF GUATEMALA.

MONUMENT TO JUAN SEBASTIÁN ELCANO, IN THE ROUNDABOUT OF THE VOLUNTARY SAILORS.

of Saint Telmo and the consulate of this country, and the **Pavilion of Morocco**, work by Gutiérrez Lescure. Next to the gardens of the Delights are the **Pavilion of Argentina**, work by Martín Noel, and the **Pavilion of Guatemala**, whose external walls are totally covered by tiles. In the Roundabout of the Volunteer Sailors (Glorieta de los Marineros Voluntarios) is a **monument to Juan Sebastián Elcano**, who disembarked in the harbour of Seville in 1522 after completing this seafarer the first trip around the world, and the **Sewing basket of the Queen (Costurero de la Reina)**,

nowadays headquarters of the Local Tourist Office, a small castle that belonged to the old gardens of the Palace of Saint Telmo. And between the Roundabout of the Sailors and the La Rábida street are the **Pavilion of United States**, work by William Templeton Johnson, headquarters of the consulate of this country; the **Pavilion of Uruguay**, work by Emilio Cravoto; the **Pavilion of Perú**, work by Manuel Piqueras, which reproduces the architecture of the Archbishop's Palace of Lima, and the **Pavilion of Chile**, today head office of the Applied Arts School.

PAVILION OF PERÚ.

SEVILLE VIEW FROM TRIANA.

The name of this famous Sevillian quarter is owed to the emperor Trajan, word which the Arabs transformed in *Tarayanah*. Populated since very ancient times, it was built up as a poor quarter of the city in the other bank of the river, joined to this side only with a pontoon bridge done with barges until 1852 when the bridge of Elizabeth ll was opened, more known as the bridge of Triana. The other bridge that connects with these quarters, the Saint Telmo's bridge, was not finished until 1931. Triana is a traditional seamen's quarter (Rodrigo de Triana, who accompanied Columbus on board of *La Pinta*, was the first European to see the American land, and here were formed the crews that departed to the New World, among them the famous *Magellan-Elcano*) and also it is known for its pottery tradition and for being the fact that many flamenco singers and bullfighters have been born here. A walk through the quarters allows to discover corners of genuine personality, like the Pelay Correa, Flota and Rocío streets, which conserve several houses of typical style of Triana. In the Antillano Campos and Saint George's streets are the main ceramic shops that so much fame have given to Triana.

One of the main streets of Triana is the **Betis street**, next to the river and full of terraces, from where you can obtain one of the most suggestive views of Seville. In the street of Purity, parallel to the Betis street, is the **Chapel of the Sailors**, built between 1759 and 1815, where the image of the Virgin of the Hope of Triana (Virgen de la Esperanza de Triana) is worshiped, image with whom the whole quarter is identified.

The main temple of Triana, as it was used as the cathedral of the quarters until the bridge of Elizabeth ll was built since this temple was used during the Holy Week by the different brotherhoods of Triana as a penance station, is the **Saint Anne's Curch**, being also one of the most oldest ones of Seville. It was founded in 1276 by Alfonso X, but totally rebuilt in the 14th century and still remodeled in the following centuries. The main retable, of Renaissance style, presents fifteen painting with scenes of the life of the Virgin, Saint Joaquin and Saint Anne, and holds in the central niche a group of sculptures from the second half of the 13th century with the images of Saint Anne, the Virgin and Baby Jesus. Other outstanding elements are the Sacramental Chapel, decorated with plaster works from the 16th century, the images of the Christ of Help, Saint Joaquín and the Mother of God of the Rosary, a Blessed Virgin attributed to Luisa Roldán, the retable of the Divine Shepherdess, and a polyptich which represents Saint Catalina with four apostles, underneath of which is a tomb decorated with ceramics done by Niculoso Pisano of 1503. Nevertheless, this church is specially known for the Font of the Gypsies, which according to the tradition bestows the gift of flamenco and a good voice for

SAINT ANNE'S CHURCH.

CHAPEL OF THE SAILORS: IMAGE OF OUR LADY OF HOPE OF TRIANA.

singing to the children that are babtized in it.

Other temples of Triana are the **church of Saint Jacinto**, in the corner of the San Jacinto and Pagés del Corro streets, in front of a little square where there is a beautiful specimen of an American rubber plant; the **church of Our Lady of the O**, from the ends of the 17th century, in the

Castilla street, and the **Carmen's Chapel**, next to the bridge of Elizabeth II, in the Altozano square, which the Sevillians call "the lighter" for its peculiar form of a lighter, a work of Aníbal González of 1926.

The **Altozano square** was restored in the 19th century after the desition to demolish the Castle of Saint George, of Arab origin and which the Catholic Monarchs gave to the Court of the Holy Service in 1482. Only the **arch** was conserved in the alley of the Inquisition, passage that connected the castle and a jetty in the river, and which was opened to avoid the condemned to be seen by the people. The place of the castle was occupied by the **Market of Triana**, while as in the square can be admired a **monument to Juan Belmonte**, a work by Venancio Blanco. Juan Belmonte (1892-1962), born in Seville, made up with Joselito the most famous couple of all times in the bullfighting world. Among other introductions that made him be considered the first bullfighter with style, he was the first one to stand still in front of the bulls, staying cool and putting up, which meant a real revolution in the art of bullfighting. Through the hole in the chest of this sculpture you can see the bullfighting ring of the Real Maestranza, in where is considered that he made his first presentation bullfight in 1910.

CARMEN'S CHAPEL AND JUAN BELMONTE MONUMENT.

MONASTERY OF SANTA MARÍA DE LAS CUEVAS.

If the Latin American Exhibition of 1929 already had an exceptional importance for Seville and it left legacies so interesting as the España and America squares, the celebration of the Universal Exhibition of 1992, whose great scene was what is known as the Isle of la Cartuja, supposed a still bigger happening. Under the slogan of "The Age of the Discoveries" and coinciding with the commemoration of the fifth centenary of the discovery of America, the Expo of Seville accommodated the pavilions of the different international organizations and of more than a hundred countries from around the world, many of which have been re-adapted for new services, it also constituted a great spectacle in which were partici-

pated the most prestigious artists and which managed to bring together thousands and thousands of visitors. On the other hand, the designation of Seville as venue of the Universal Exhibition entailed the definitive takeoff of the city towards the new century undertaking big public works as the construction of new bridges that cross both banks of the river Guadalquivir, the Station of Santa Justa, which presently concentrates the whole railroad transit of the city, starting to operate the High Speed Train (AVE), the new airport and several surrounding roads.

Previously in this huge area delimited by the two arms of the Guadalquivir, from there its denomination of isle, hardly existed anything except the old

monastery of Santa María de las Cuevas, more known as La Cartuja of Seville, a historical monument built in the 15th century. Here stayed in more than one occasion Cristopher Columbus, who shared with the Carthusian monks his geographical theories and where he prepared part of the adventure that would take him to America in 1492, and it also served as accommodation to the kings that passed through Seville. The monks stayed at the premises till 1836, when they were expelled as a result of the law of Confiscation. A great part of the works of art that it kept, among which many of the most important creations of the Sevillian School, are shown in the Museum of Fine Arts. Between 1841 and

1982 it housed a ceramics factory, after which the building was restored to convert it in headquarters of the Royal Pavilion of the Universal Exhibition. Of the old buildings of the monastery we have to mention the Prior's House, the chapel of Outside (capilla de Afuera), the Chapterhouse and a Mudejar cloister. Nowadays La Cartuja of Seville accommodates the Andalusian Institute of Historical Patrimony, the Vice-Chancellorship of the International University of Andalusia and the **Andalusian Center of Contemporary Art (CAAC)**, which organizes temporary exhibitions and has a representative collection of works of art of the most prominent contemporary Andalusian artists.

Located between the monastery and the Triana quarters, the so called **Espacio Cultural Puerta de Triana** includes offers such as the Omnimax Spacial Cinema, the Pavilion of the Navigation, a catamaran, the ship *Victoria* (copy of the vessels from the 16th century) and the sightseeing tower of 1992, which allows to have a board perspective of Seville and all this new area.

But surely the ludic space of the Isle of la Cartuja that receives most visits is the theme park **Magic Island (Isla Mágica)**, in which are recreated the trips and feats of the explorers that in the 16th century departed from Seville towards the New World. The park also includes a gigantic and spectacular roller coaster called Jaguar, and another one of water, the Anaconda, among many other attractions.

Behind the Isla Mágica, in the Scientific and Technologic Park of Cartuja 93, or **Sevilla Tecnópolis**, several pavilions left from the Exhibition accommodate today the head offices of various companies and several centers of the University of Seville. Among them we have to mention the building of the World Trade Center for its advanced bioclimatical technology.

AERIAL VIEW OF THE "ISLA MÁGICA" PARK AND OF SEVILLA TECNÓPOLIS.

"ISLA MÁGICA" FUNFAIR.

The Isla de la Cartuja is also a center of periodic shows, that take place in the **Auditorium**, in open air and with a capacity for 6,000 spectators, and in the **Central Theater**.

To finish, in the northern part of the Isle we can find the **Park of Alamillo**, which with its 894,000 m^2 of gardens has become the main green lung of Seville, and several sports installations, among which is the **Olympic Stadium**, a work done by the architects Antonio Cruz and Antonio Ortiz, who built it beneath ground level to avoid the environmental impact and which has capacity for 60,000 seated spectators.

Gardens of the Espacio Cultural Puerta de Triana and Olympic Stadium.

RAMÓN SÁNCHEZ PIZJUÁN STADIUM.

BENITO VILLAMARÍN STADIUM.

Seville enjoys of a great amount of parks and gardens. Besides the already mentioned of María Luisa, Murillo and Alamillo, we have to mention the park of **Arboreto de El Carambolo** and the **Park of the Princes**. The first one is located in the El Carambolo hill and gathers approximately about 500 different specimen of plants in a space of four hectares of gardens. The second one is in the Los Remedios quarters and it is composed of board grasslands and paths lined with orange trees.

The **Palace of Exhibitions and Congresses** is situated in the area known as Seville East and it consists of a central building, two side buildings and three big pavilions for exhibitions, besides a great area with gardens for events to be held in open air.

Seville has two football stadiums. The **Ramón Sánchez Pizjuán Stadium**, in the Nervión quarters, is the head quarter of the Sevilla Fútbol Club. From the building stands out the facade, with an enormous mosaic of 30 meters high with the shield of the club in the middle, and surrounding it, several shields of clubs around the world. The other stadium, headquarters of the Real Betis Balompié, is the **Benito Villamarín Stadium** (Avenida de la Palmera s/n).

SANTIPONCE: PLANETARIUM MOSAIC AND PASSAGE OF THE ROMAN CIRCUS, IN ITÁLICA.

SANTIPONCE

The village of Santiponce, situated only 7 km from Seville going Northeast, has two main attractions for the visitor: the Archaeological Monuments of Itálica and the monastery of San Isidoro del Campo.

The village of Santiponce was raised at the end of the XVI on top of what used to be the "vetus urbs" or the old city of **Itálica**, while the remains that can be visited nowadays correspond essentially to the "nova urbs" or new city which was created in the 2nd century. Itálica has its origin in the city founded by Scipio the African in 206 BC as retirement of his troops after winning the Carthaginian general Asdrúbal nearby grounds, calling it Itáli-

ca after the place they came from. As time went by, Itálica became a prosperous urban center. The ruins we can admire today show the ancient trace of the city, remains of mosaics and sculptures, but above all impress the theater and the amphitheater, this last one of elliptical trace and a capacity for 25,000 spectators.

Itálica was the birthplace of Marco Ulpio Trajano (53-117), the first Roman emperor born in a province of the Empire, and of his successor and adoptive son, Publio Aelio Adriano (76-138), designer of the monumentality that this city arrived to have. A statue of this last mentioned figure stands the higher part of Itálica. The abandonment and the sacking

that it suffered in following centuries marked the history of Itálica, converting it in a ghost city of its glorious past. In a small museum are shown several pieces found in the premises, although the most valuable ones are kept in the Archaeological Museum of Seville.

The **monastery of San Isidoro del Campo**, which has been recently restored, was founded in 1301 for the monks of Cistercian order. Don Alonso Pérez de Guzmán was who finantiated the construction. In 1431 it passed to accommodate a community of monks of the order of Jeronimo, who stayed there till 1836, date of the Confiscation Law. At the beginning of the 20th century the community of monks returned, but nowadays it is unoccupied and can be visited. It has a beautiful Mudejar cloister and important works of art, to mention a retable of Martínez Montañés, done between 1609 and 1613, and the tombs of the founders of the monastery, Guzmán el Bueno and his wife Doña María Coronel.

NATURAL PARK OF SIERRA NORTE

It has an extension of 164,480 hectares and it comprehends the area of Sierra Morena that adjoines the provinces of Huelva and Córdoba and the Community of Extremadura. The meadowed hills dominate this landscape, where man has eliminated the original Mediterranean bushes for the exploitation of the cork oak trees and the holm oak for stockbreeding purposes, specially for the breeding of the Iberian pig. The park also hides corners of suggestive beauty as is the place where is the source of the river Huéznar, with leafy elms, alders, ashes, willows and hazels and two fishing preserves, and the old mining settlement of El Cerro del Hierro, next to which raises a limestone massif in where the effect of the rain and the mining activity (which lasted until the 70's) have originated an original landscape which contrasts with the rest of the mountain range. In some areas, specially in the higher ones, there are access restrictions in periods of nesting of the imperial eagle and the black stork, the most significative birds of the park. In general, as it is a cool place in the summer, during the last years it has converted in to a refuge for many Sevillians. Its main villages are **Cazalla de la Sierra** and **Constantina**, where there are information centers concerning the park and these villages are very known for the manufacture of anisettes and liqueurs and the production of sweets and 'ambrosías' (a type of sweet custard), which are another of the main economical activities of the zone.

REFECTORY OF THE MONASTERY OF SAN ISIDORO DEL CAMPO.

CARMONA: SAN FERNANDO SQUARE.

CARMONA

Situated about 25 km from Seville, Carmona is of great touristic interest for its monumental richness. Of its Roman past it conserves the rests of the wall, the amphitheater and the necropolis. During the Arab period the city managed to reach great splendour. To this period correspond the foundations of the Fortress of king Peter I the Cruel (one of which wings is today a National Tourist Parador, a state-owned hotel) and the old central area which, in spite of the later extensions, maintains a marked oriental atmosphere.

CARMONA: CHURCH OF SANTA MARÍA.

During the 17th and 18th centuries Carmona was filled with convents and palaces. What concerns small palaces, the Palace of Aguilar and the Palace of Rueda are beautiful exponents of the Baroque architecture. From the religious buildings stand out the church of Santa María (built in the 15th century in the place of the old main mosque, of which is conserved the ablutions patio), the convent of Santa Clara and the church of San Felipe, both of Mudejar style, or the church of San Pedro, whose tower reminds the Giralda of Seville.

MUSEUM OF
THE CITY
OF CARMONA
IN AN OLD
PALACE AND
TYPICAL
STREET.

CARMONA:
WALLS OF THE
FORTRESS.

PARTIAL VIEW OF ÉCIJA.

ÉCIJA

The main charm of Écija is in its urban historical buildings, white houses with railings in the windows and ocher coloured roofs. It has, besides, a big number of churches and manor houses. Écija is also known as the "city of the towers", since it has a total number of eleven, being the one of the church of San Juan the most beautiful, and "the frying pan of Andalusia", for the high temperatures that are achieved in summer. Among its monuments stand out the Palace of Peñaflor or "house of the long balconies", the convent of the Teresas, that used to be a manor

ÉCIJA: PEÑAFLOR AND BENAMEJÍ PALACES.

ÉCIJA: SANTA CRUZ SQUARE AND DETAIL OF THE SAN JUAN'S CHURCH TOWER.

TWO VIEWS OF THE COLLEGIATE OF SANTA MARÍA, IN OSUNA.

house, and the Palace of Benamejí, today headquarter of the Local Museum.

OSUNA

Village of Iberian origin, Osuna lived its biggest period of splendour when Philip II bestowed the title of duke of Osuna to the duke of Ureña. From this period, 16th century, date its main monuments, among which stand out the Colegiata de Santa María de la Asunción (which keeps inside an excellent art gallery), the University and the Pantheom of the dukes of Osuna. The Tower of the Water, from the 12th century, accommodates nowadays the Ar-

chaeological Museum, with Iberian, Roman and Visigothic vestiges. From those remote times are also conserved, at the outskirts the remains of a Roman circus and necropolis.

It is recommended to extend this visit to neighbour village of **Estepa**, very famous for its delicious 'mantecados' and 'polvorones' (floury sweets made with lard the first ones and with almonds the second ones). The old quarters, with narrow streets and railings in the windows, is very pleasant to walk. Among its monuments we have to mention the baroque church of Carmen, the Tower of the Victory (18th century) and the

OLD UNIVERSITY OF
OSUNA.

OSUNA: FACADE OF
THE CHAPTER
COLLEGIATE AND
PALACE OF THE
CEPEDA.

CASTLE OF ALCALÁ DE GUADAIRA.

church of Santa María de la Asunción, built on top of an old mosque.

ALCALÁ DE GUADAIRA

In days gone by it was also known as Alcalá de los Panaderos (Alcalá of the Bakers), while it supplied bread to Seville. It is a very close city to the capital, dominated by a big Almohade period castle (12th century). Very well conserved, it has an irregular floor, two patios and eleven towers. For its strategic position, it always served as bastion for the defence of the metropoly. Other interesting places of Alcalá are many water mills, in majority Mudejar, the castle of Marchenilla and the churches of Santiago, San Sebastián and San Miguel.

MARCHENA

From the Arab period, **Marchena** maintains the urban layout and part of the walls, in which still remains a door called Arch of Rose (Arco de la Rosa). The 15th and 16th centuries, with the support of the dukes of Arcos, to which domain it belonged, represented a prodigious period in architecture. The disappeared palace of the dukes of Arcos was in the Ducal Square, main point of interest of this village. In the palace was the tower of the old castle, the called Mudejar Patio and the Chapterhouses. From the various churches of Marchena stand out the church of San Juan Bautista, of Gothic-Mudejar style, with a magnificent retable from the 16th century, the church of San

Miguel, Mudejar although very transformed in the 18th century, and the church of Mota, built between the 15th and 16th centuries.

MAIRENA DEL ALCOR

This nice village owes its present layout to the Arabs. To that period corresponds also the Castle of Luna, later reformed by Rodrigo Ponce de León, marquis-duke of Cádiz, as headquarters of his troops. It is conserved in a very good state and an archaeological museum has been installed there. Other interesting places are the Church of Asunción, of Mudejar trace and the chapels of the Christ of the Prison (Cristo de la Cárcel) and of San Sebastián.

MARCHENA: DUCAL SQUARE.

MAIRENA DEL ALCOR: CASTLE OF LUNA.

UTRERA: REMAINS OF THE CASTLE, SANTA MARÍA DE LA MESA'S CHURCH AND CASTLE TOWER OF LOPERA.

UTRERA

As many Andalusian villages, the old quarters of this town situated South of Seville preserves a marked oriental atmosphere. Its origins, nevertheless, are much more remote, being one of the most important towns of the Bética. After the definitive Christian conquest at the end of the 14th century, Utrera went through a long period of struggles between feudal lords. Peace did not arrive until the XVI century, after finishing the Reconquest. From its monuments, we have to mention the impressive ruins of its castle, (from the 14th century, with alterations of the 15th and 16th centuries), The Castle Tower de la Lopera (14th century), which was destinated to the defence of the frontiers between Seville and Granada), the church of Santiago el Mayor (14th century), the church of Santa María de la Mesa (15th century), the convent of the Purísima Concepción (16th century) and the Hospital de la Santa Resurrección (17th century).

EL CORONIL

The Castle of Aguzaderas, of Arab origin, is the most notable building of this town of the South of the province. After the Christian conquest, it belonged to the House of Esquivel, governors of Andalusia, who improved it in 1381 in order to exercise more pressure against the Arabs of Morón. Later it became property of the House of Medinaceli, which in the 20th century gave it to the City Hall. El Coronil besides includes another castle in the old quarters, also built by the Arabs in the XI century and rebuilt after the Reconquest. Also of interest are the churches of Our Lady of Comfort (Nuestra Señora de la Consolación), of Mudejar trace, and of Our Lady of the Remedies (Nuestra Señora de los Remedios), from the 18th century.

EL CORONIL: CASTLE OF THE AGUZADERAS.

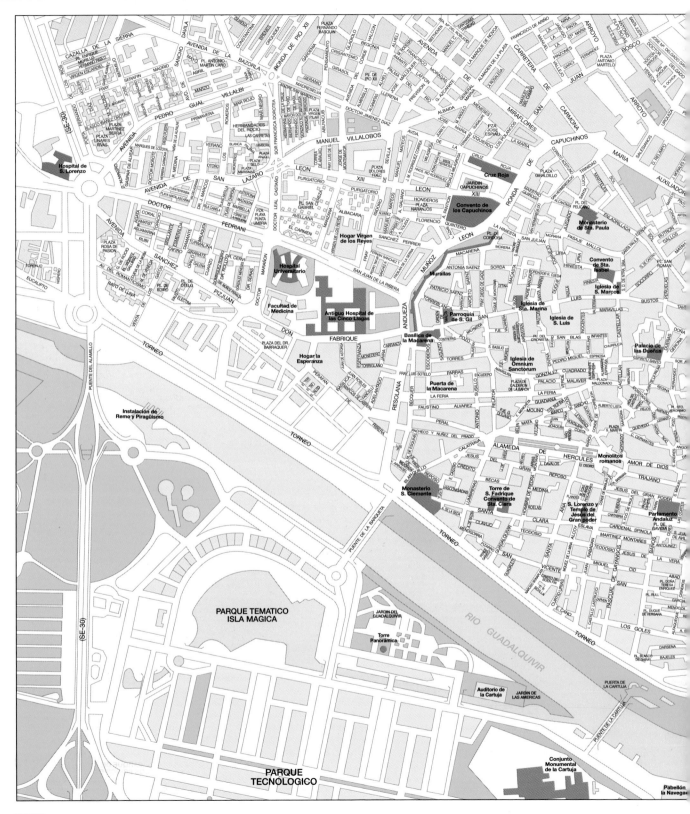

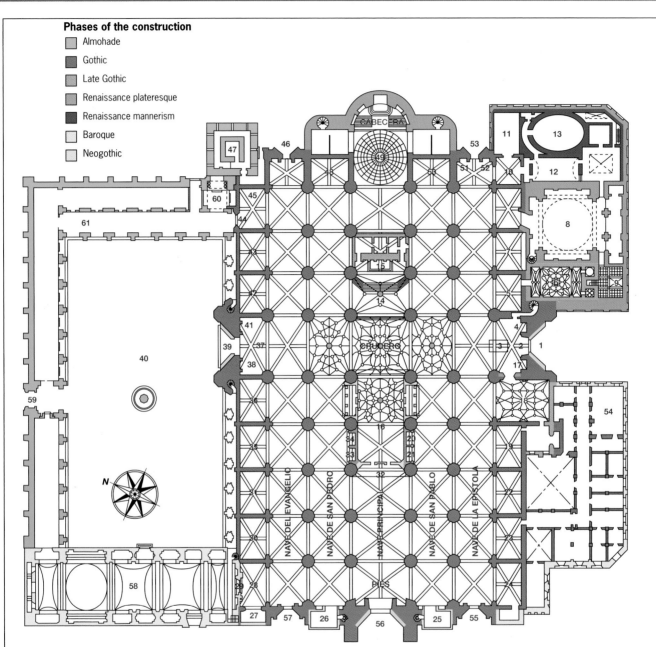

Phases of the construction

- Almohade
- Gothic
- Late Gothic
- Renaissance plateresque
- Renaissance mannerism
- Baroque
- Neogothic

1- Prince's Door. 2- Southern Arm of the crossing. 3- Culumbus' Tomb. 4- Altar of the Piedad. 5- Chapel of Dolores. 6- Sacristy of the Chalices. 7- San Andres' Chapel 8- Main Sacristy. 9- Patio of the Casa de Cuentas. 10- Marshal's Chapel. 11- Room of the Ornaments. 12- Antechapter. 13- Chapterhouse Room. 14- Main Chapel. 15- Main Retable. 16- Choir. 17- Concepción's Altar. 18- Chapel of the Antigua. 19- San Hermenegildo's Chapel. 20- Concepción Chica's Chapel. 21- Encarnación's Chapel. 22- San Jose's Chapel. 23- Santa Ana's Chapel. 24- San Laureano's Chapel. 25- San Isidoro's Chapel. 26- San Leandro's Chapel. 27- Chapel of the Angustias. 28- Replica of the Giraldillo. 29- Facade of the Sagrario's church. 30- San Antonio's Chapel. 31- Chapel of Nuestra Señora de la Consolación de los Doce Apóstoles. 32- Transchoir. 33- Chapel of the Star (Capilla de la Estrella). 34- Chapel of San Gregorio. 35- Santiago's Chapel. 36- San Francisco's Chapel. 37- Northern arm of the Crossing. 38- Chapel of Bethlehem. 39- Door of the Concepción. 40- Patio of the Orange Trees. 41- Asunción's Altar. 42- Chapel of the Maidens. 43- Chapel of the Evangelists. 44- Door of the Lizard. 45- Pilar's Chapel. 46- Door of the Stakes (Puerta de los Palos). 47- Giralda. 48- San Pedro's Chapel. 49- Royal Chapel. 50- Chapel of the Concepción Grande. 51- Santa Barbara's Altar. 52- Altar of the Santas Justa and Rufina. 53- Door of the Little Bells. 54- Archive and Offices. 55- Door of the Crib. 56- Asunción's Door. 57- Door of the Baptism. 58- Sagrario's Church. 59- Door of the Forgiveness. 60- Virgin of the Granada's Chapel. 61- Chapterhouse and Colombina Library.